Headstrong

The ultimate guide to reducing lapses in concentration, building confidence and finding your zone on the volleyball court.

Brooke Rundle

2nd Edition 2020

CONTENTS

CONTENTS 2
COACHES TESTIMONIALS 3
CREDITS 6
DISCLAIMER 7
COPYRIGHT 8
DOWNLOAD THE FREE WORKBOOK 9
A FEW NOTES TO THE READER 10
THE 6 HEADSTRONG MINDSET TRAINING
MODULES 12
INTRODUCTION 14
MODULE 1 : CONCENTRATION 20
MODULE 2 : CONFIDENCE 32
MODULE 3 : MINDSET 48
MODULE 4 : THE ZONE 64
MODULE 5 : TEAMWORK 82
MODULE 6 : SELF-CARE 110
CLOSING INSPIRATION 126
HEADSTRONG™ MINDSET TRAINING PROGRAM
.... 132
ABOUT THE AUTHOR 133
ACKNOWLEDGMENTS 135
Endnotes 137

COACHES TESTIMONIALS

AL SCATES, Coached the UCLA Mens Volleyball Team to 19 NCAA Titles.

"Both the experienced and the novice will improve their performance by reading Brooke Rundle's guide to concentration and confidence building. All those who have been closely associated with the sport of volleyball will recognize that her techniques will help you improve on the court and in life."

BROOK COULTER, Associate Head Coach Colorado State University 2012-2015.

"Rundle gave a presentation on the Headstrong principles and strategies at CSU's team camp in 2015. Our coaches found the Headstrong techniques to declutter the mind, build confidence and prioritize improvement over accomplishment extremely helpful and practical for players and coaches alike. The guide offers actionable tips for practice and a game plan to help volleyball players improve their mental game. I highly recommend grabbing a copy of this book and booking her for a speaking engagement at your camp or club."

LESLIE FLORES-CLOUD, Head Volleyball Coach Eastern Washington University

"Headstrong- is my new favorite volleyball book. Not only should every athlete read it but every coach as well. The book dives into simple techniques to enhance your mental toughness. As a coach, I have changed how I talk with athletes and positively motivate them. Brooke does a great job of sharing the struggles and triumphs of the volleyball greats. This book has volleyball history and toughness all rolled into one."

Rachelle Sherden, Head Volleyball Coach Gustavus Adolphus College and 2015 AVCA Central Region Coach of the Year.

"I feel so fortunate that our team had the opportunity to work with Brooke during our "virtual" spring season. Headstrong 2.0 and the team workbook proved to be hugely beneficial for our athletes and our team as a whole. Through the six modules and team sessions our athletes learned simple, yet powerful volleyball-specific strategies to grow their mental game in practice and competition. On top of that, the athletes' relationships became infinitely stronger after they learned more about each other and worked together through each module and team session. I feel like the team made leaps and bounds forward together, even more so than if we would have had a "normal" spring season. The Headstrong sessions exceeded all of our expectations and we are very grateful for the experience!"

JEFF MEEKER, Head Volleyball Coach Cornell College and 7-Time Conference Coach of the Year.

"This book is not just another tool for coaches, rather is it an entire tool box to inspire growth in our athletes, provide a more positive experience and become better coaches. Brooke's unique and diverse experiences provide keen insight into how we can help our athletes become mentally strong in volleyball and beyond."

JENNIFER JACOBS, Head Volleyball Coach Augustana University and Diversity & Inclusion Speaker.

"In this day in age - a social media selfie obsessed world - it has become extremely difficult for coaches to create a team culture that thrives on the "we," not the "me" mentality. Brooke Rundle captures that essence in her book Headstrong. My favorite module, module 5 - Teamwork lays it all out there on the table for teams to address with each other. It takes a bold leader to truly address gossip, and Headstrong gives coaches and players the tools to face it in a safe and productive way. Additionally, the section on implicit bias is the first time I have ever seen that topic addressed specific to volleyball. Headstrong gives us tangible examples, real life situations, and is a fantastic how - to guide to help coaches and teams navigate a relevant complex concept."

CREDITS

Cover image of Courtney Thompson playing in Rexona Superliga match in Rio de Janeiro, Brazil contributed by Ricardo Haleck.

DISCLAIMER

Although the author and publisher have made every effort to ensure that the information in this book was correct at the time of publication, the author and publisher do not assume and hereby disclaim any liability to any party for any loss, damage, or disruption caused by errors or omissions, whether such errors or omissions result from negligence, accident, or any other cause.

COPYRIGHT

All rights reserved. No part of this publication may be reproduced, distributed, or transmitted in any form or by any means, including photocopying or other electronic mechanical methods, without the prior written permission of the publisher, except in the case of brief quotations embodied in reviews and certain other non-commercial uses permitted by copyright law.

Copyright © 2016 by Brooke Rundle
1st Edition Published: January 2016
Edited by Wesley Dean

Copyright © 2020 by Brooke Rundle
2nd Edition Published: June 2020
Edited by Hannah Vanderlan
https://headstrongmindset.com/workbook/

DOWNLOAD THE FREE WORKBOOK

I have created a free workbook for players to do while reading this book. The workbook contains activities, training tools and additional resources for each of the 6 mindset training modules covered in the book: concentration, confidence, mindset, the zone, teamwork and self-care.

To get the free workbook, just head over to my website at http://headstrongmindset.com/workbook/ and drop in your email. I'll send it to you right away so that you can do the activities on your own or with your teammates.

A FEW NOTES TO THE READER

My role as the Director of Marketing & Development with Bring It Promotions volleyball agency has allowed me the opportunity to work closely with college teams at the Division I, II, III and NAIA levels. I've hosted foreign volleyball tours with an emphasis on team building for dozens of top collegiate teams including: Creighton University, University of Northern Iowa, Princeton University, Missouri State, Gannon University, Emory University, Drake University and many more.

While traveling with these teams internationally, I've had the opportunity to peel back the curtain, step inside the huddle and listen to deep and oftentimes vulnerable conversations between players and coaches. It's also opened the doors for me to interview top collegiate, professional and national team coaches around the world.

This unique experience has taught me common patterns of behavior and strategies that universally unlock the potential of individual players and teams. No matter which team I'm working with or where in the world I travel to, I have found that the best teams, in addition to developing technical skills and physical strength, always dedicate time to mindset training.

I wrote this book and created the Headstrong™ Mindset Training Program specifically for volleyball players. It's a tool for serious players and teams who want to take their game to the next level. In the book and accompanying workbook, I've boiled my content and strategies down to 6 key modules. This book and accompanying workbook are designed for players to read and work through either individually or together as a team.

Since I identify as a woman and most of the volleyball teams I work with are women's teams, I've written the book from a woman's point of view. However, the techniques, strategies and tools are universal.

Throughout the book I intentionally ignore grammar at times and purposefully use volleyball slang. The informality of the text is intended to help players relate. I wrote this book with the same voice I coach and play with on the volleyball court.

THE 6 HEADSTRONG MINDSET TRAINING MODULES

1. **CONCENTRATION**

   Be aware of when you lose focus and redirect attention. Create a focus cue. Eye-sequencing, a powerful concentration tool on the court.

2. **CONFIDENCE**

   Let go of mistakes immediately. Negative thought replacement. Approach competition with clear tactical plans. Train harder than anyone.

3. **MINDSET**

   Adopt a growth mindset. Change your court vocabulary. Always compete.

4. **THE ZONE**

   Establish a dedicated pre-game routine. Practice mindfulness. Create your own visualization script. Get out of your head and into your body.

5. **TEAMWORK**

   Shift your world view from scarcity to abundance. Make a pledge to not gossip about teammates. Develop systems of communication. Create a culture of belonging.

Dismantle implicit bias.

6. **SELF-CARE**

    Yoga as a training tool. Rest, the unexpected key to resilience. Embrace body positivity. Find balance.

INTRODUCTION

Pass.

Set.

Hit.

Block.

You know how to execute each of these individual skills. You know the footwork and you know the technique. You may even know dozens of setting, serve-receive, and transition hitting drills to improve the various aspects of the game as well as countless potential play scenarios that your team may face in competition.

But this book is about the inner game. The one played inside your head. The one each player plays alone, independent of others and indifferent to the coaches on the bench.

Every player on the court must prepare for their own battle. These mental battles rage on at the end of practice, at the beginning of a game, and at the end-line when serving for match point.

Sometimes the battlefield is calm and the voice is quiet. Sometimes it is chaotic and the voice is loud.

There are times when the inner voice distracts, doubts, chastises, lapses in concentration and even abuses oneself.

And there are times when the inner voice focuses like a laser beam, believes in dreams beyond reach, and cultivates a winning confidence that is contagious on the court.

The inner voice always has something to say. It's constantly calling out and it resonates louder than the shouts of your teammates and coaches combined.

In a sport that's so often won by just two points, the mental game of volleyball is the difference between winning and losing. The death of side-out scoring inflated the cost of each point.

In the world of rally scoring, mental errors are significantly more difficult to overcome. Focus, confidence, and mental clarity are vital to peak performance.

In the pursuit of victory, there is no room for

nervousness. Self-doubt has no place on the court. Self-condemnation serves only the opponent. And, whether coaches want to hear it or not, an overload of technical information is often damaging and distracting during competition.

Your mindset is the difference-maker. It is the difference between burying the ball into the block or wiping it off the hands of the opponent. It's the difference between pushing the serve to zone 5 or attacking the left-back passer, forcing them to take a step deep into the sideline to receive an aggressively targeted serve. It's the difference between winning and losing.

If you are serious about winning and committed to taking your team to the next level, you must commit to training your mind. This is no less necessary than or different from physical training and is just as important as each individual volleyball skill.

So how do you train your mind? How do you control the inner voice? How can you make it work *for* you instead of *against* you? How do you unlock your highest potential? How do you stay connected to your teammates when the pressure is on?

Whether it's your very first practice or game 5 with the

season on the line, there are practical tips and tools that can be used to maintain a lucid state of awareness and an unflappable self-confidence.

Low self-confidence on the court is not a permanent state of being. Lapses in concentration are something you can train your mind against. Finding your zone on the volleyball court takes practice, not luck. The right mental training can change your performance on the court. Good communication and connectedness among teammates starts before you step foot on the court.

What's in the book:

I've interviewed dozens of players and coaches at the highest level of volleyball to create the ultimate guide for players and coaches on mental training. The book is divided into 6 modules and I've packed them full of confidence-building and team-building strategies, as well as practical tips to help players maintain their concentration and communication under pressure on the court.

In Module 1, I kick it off with 3 practical tips to help you clear your mind of distractions on the court. These strategies are highly volleyball-oriented and applicable for players at every level.

Then in Module 2, I dive into 4 proven strategies to help players build confidence and self-esteem while practicing and developing skills. The foundation for each of the concepts in this section have been developed based on the advice of expert coaches and top level players.

Module 3 is a mind-map for adopting a growth-mindset on the volleyball court (and in life). Changing your mindset can be difficult and often messy, but that's why you're reading this book. Think of the information contained in this module as the foundation for mental fitness. You'll find it especially useful in matches too.

In Module 4, I zero in on specific strategies and tools that you can use to prepare your mind for competition. If the pressure of competition causes your muscles to tighten up, then you're going to find this section especially useful. Before beginning this module, take a deep breath, forget about your to-do list, and read with an open mind.

Module 5 is like playing queen of the court, it's everyone's favorite part of practice. Here I focus on the key factors to building and strengthening the relationships with your teammates to reach your team's potential.

Module 6 is a straight forward and comprehensive plan that teaches you how to achieve a sense of inner peace and resilience. This module is intentionally a little more gentle and vulnerable than the others. The lessons here are highly applicable both on and off the court.

Throughout the book I've scattered real-life stories and experiences from volleyball experts covering their journey to learn and master the game. While many of the contributors will be well known to you, others may be new. The common thread binding these anecdotes is clear – each unique story holds a valuable volleyball lesson worth preserving.

Finally, don't forget to download the free workbook of easy to follow strategies to improve your mental game. I made it especially to help you implement the techniques discussed in this book. You can do the workbook on your own, or together with your teammates.

This is your secret weapon to reduce lapses in concentration, build confidence, and find your zone on the volleyball court. So open your mind and embrace it. It's time to get started on creating the positive change you want to see on the court.

MODULE 1 : CONCENTRATION

"If there were just one thing I would always tell my players, it would be that no matter what's happening on the court, keep your head up and just focus on the next play."

Al Scates, Coached the UCLA Men's Volleyball Team to 19 NCAA Titles.

It is a battle to maintain your undivided focus on the ball for the entire rally, let alone an entire game or match. Coaches are shouting strategies for the next play or yelling constructive criticism from the bench. Fans are cheering on your team and heckling your opponents. Parents, friends and partners might catch your eye triggering a lapse in your attention. Losing focus during competition is very common and totally natural. Most of the time, we're not even aware of when or how often our attention breaks.

In an interview on the *Undivided Attention Podcast,* Gloria Mark, a professor of informatics at the University of California at Irvine, reported that the median length of time people can hold their attention in front of a computer screen or phone is 40 seconds[1]. That means most people break concentration and switch actions about every 40 seconds when they are in front of a screen. Just think about how you switch back and forth on your phone between TikTok, Snapchat, Instagram, YouTube, Facebook, or just regular old text messages, phone calls and emails.

Now consider how long the average length of a volleyball rally lasts. According to a study performed by the FIVB, the average rally duration for volleyball teams at the Olympic level is 7.3 seconds for women and 5.5 seconds for men[2]. While the average length of a volleyball rally in NCAA Division I typically lasts anywhere between 13 and 60 seconds[3]. However, there's tons of examples of volleyball rallies exceeding a minute at the collegiate level, especially when the stakes are high. In October of 2019, Nebraska's 50 second rally with Michigan State at 9-9 in the 4th set was one of college volleyball's plays of the week. In a Big Ten volleyball match up between Nebraska and Illinois in 2015, there was a one-minute, 12 second rally in the second set[4]. And in October of 2019, the NCAA's number one play of the week was a 1.55 minute rally won by North Texas[5].

While the factors impacting your concentration on the volleyball court differ greatly from those distracting you on the phone, if you're used to only concentrating for short bursts of 40 second increments, it's going to impact your ability to sustain concentration during match play. To be a successful volleyball player, you need to be able to retain focus during a rally for more than 40 seconds a time.

Developing a mindful approach towards playing is the key to maintaining concentration and being present on the volleyball court. Being present on the court means not worrying about the last play, or whether or not you're going to win the game 3 points from now, but instead staying completely focused on the here and now. Players that operate in the present are much more likely to be able to read what is happening across the net and react accordingly.

Attention management is a skill that can be developed and improved. But if you don't train your mind to work for you, then you may find it working against you. Improving your concentration on the court is critical to reaching your potential. So how do we declutter our minds from these distractions?

The same way you improve the consistency of every other technical skill in the game of volleyball…with lots of practice. Repetition after repetition. Athletes should treat the mind as a muscle that needs to be exercised and strengthened like every other. Most mistakes on the volleyball court are caused by lack of focus. Improving your concentration is the key to performing at your best under pressure during competition.

Let's take a look at a few proven strategies to harness the power of your mind.

1. Be aware of when you lose focus and redirect your attention.

How would you rate your ability to stay focused in between points?

The gap between serves is when players are most vulnerable to "spacing out" or having a mental lapse in concentration. It's the moment when you have a chance to catch your breath and get back into ready-position but it's also enough time for you to listen to the crowd, and to overthink strategy, input from coaches, and the importance of the next point.

The break in the action allows players' minds to drift. Focus can wander to what they have to do after the match or what somebody said to them earlier that day. These tertiary concerns can be triggered by anything and can severely impact your ability to concentrate.

It's critical to be aware of *when* you have a tendency to lose focus during practice or competition. Recognizing the signs can change the momentum and direction of the moment and can help you avoid mental errors that cost valuable points. Each point saved could be the difference between winning and losing.

The best strategy to combat concentration loss on the

court is to take an honest inventory of your biggest distractions. Familiarizing yourself with the enemy is key to combating it. Create a list of the events which distract you during practice. Carefully evaluate the reasons for thoughts that have derailed your concentration in past matches.

After a mistake, do you continue to beat yourself up after the play has ended? Do comments from a teammate or coach impact your emotions? Does a parent in the stands make you nervous by adding extra pressure during matches? Or possibly, is there an aspect of your personal life that invisibly creeps onto the court?

Every item on your list of distractions is an obstacle that must be overcome. By naming and becoming aware of your personal distractions, you can learn to train your mind to view these distractions as signposts and reminders to refocus on the next play.

Sometimes the most valuable thing you can do as a team leader is to bring your teammates attention back to the ball.

2. Create a focus cue.

Every time the ball hits the ground, a player has responsibilities – rotate to the next service position, evaluate the opponent, determine the offensive or defensive strategy for the next point. Every second that passes presents an opportunity to break concentration. On, off. On, off. Around and around we go.

Every play has a different tempo. Every rotation has different players at the net and in the back row, every rotation has a new face. Every play is a point. As pressure builds throughout the match, concentration can wane and mindfulness can be lost. The player's mind can overthink everything.

Ask yourself if this sounds like a familiar scenario:

You're down by two points late in the match and you've got to put pressure on the other team with your serve.

Your coach signals an aggressive service zone.

Your palms start to sweat. The muscles in your neck and core become tense. Your heart rate increases.

Your mind starts to wander to the consequences of a negative outcome and doubts about the strength of your abilities creep in.

Deep down inside, you're nervous. You're nervous because you believe your next action will determine the result of the match.

For most players, accuracy and timing has a tendency to break down under pressure. From their toss to their footwork, everything feels out of sync. This leads to a sudden loss of confidence which severely diminishes the ability to concentrate.

I want to share a serving technique I've used throughout my entire career and shared with dozens of players that I've coached.

Would you believe that putting your forefinger on the valve of the volleyball and taking a deep breath before you serve can radically increase your concentration and therefore improve the accuracy of your serve?

It sounds so simple. Any player at any age can do this, and yet it takes discipline to develop this patient habit in practice and in games. It's so easy to rush your serve while thinking about the last play or worrying about the next one.

Finding the valve on the volleyball when going back to serve forces your mind to focus on a fixed point. It's not really about the valve, it's about establishing something consistent. Something connected to the moment, something constant and familiar that doesn't change regardless of the score or setting.

The focus point could be a tangible item or mantra to focus your mind's eye upon. It could be something stationary on the volleyball court like the ten foot line or the 3rd red stripe on the left antenna. Or it could be a series of broken down technical cues for a specific skill that you've trained repeatedly in practice.

For a setter it might be: pivot (left foot, right foot), high hands, quick release. For a hitter it could be: elbow up, shoulder back, reach, snap.

It's got to be something the player can come back to after every play and lock-in on. It's one's mental ready-position.

It doesn't matter what you focus on. The key is establishing a focal point that triggers heightened concentration through a dedicated ritual. Once cued, you should consciously re-establish your attention to the present moment. Nerves can sabotage performance if you let them. In the heat of battle, a concentration cue will alleviate pressure and increase concentration.

3. Eye sequencing, a powerful concentration tool on the court.

Eye-sequencing is the calculated eye movement patterns when the ball is in motion. It's a fancy phase for organizing what you should be looking at during the play.

Coaches often refer to eye-sequencing as "scanning" or simply "reading" the opponents across the net.

Developing a fluid and repeatable eye-sequencing practice is one of the most powerful mental training habits a player can cultivate in volleyball. It's especially useful on defense to help players identify where the ball is going. Players need to be aware of which cues to look for so you can learn to anticipate where your opponent is going to hit the ball. Ball, setter, ball, hitter is the eye sequence I like to use for blocking and playing defense[6].

A typical eye-sequence for a backcourt defender might look like this:

1. Track the <u>ball</u> when the opposing team receives the serve.
2. Read the <u>setter</u> for directional clues or 'tells' to determine which hitter will receive the set on the

next touch.

3. Track the <u>ball</u> again when it leaves the setter's hands.

4. Read the attacking <u>hitter</u>'s arm-swing for signals giving away the direction of the attack (off-speed, tip, power-swing cross court, or down the line).

Creating and practicing a clear eye-sequencing strategy is especially helpful for players who struggle with concentration as well as for those learning how to read hitters. It's easy to get lost on the court when a player follows or chases the ball rather than studying your competition and predicting what will happen next. If you always feel like you're one step behind in the play, then you're probably not reading your opponents.

The setter is often ignored during an intense rally even though she is giving away useful clues as to where the ball is going next. Most players get so focused on the quality of their own performance, that they overlook the importance of reading their opponents and anticipating the next play.

Players often struggle to identify the front row blockers or hitters across the net on any given rally. This is clearly evident when blockers jump to defend a back row setter, or when a setter runs the offense into the opponent's strongest blocker as opposed to a clearly weaker or shorter player on a different side of the court.

Identifying and practicing eye-sequence patterns will not only improve your team's defense, but also the scope of player focus. Zeroing in on specific opposing players across the net, deciphering body language, and studying 'tells' will help you to anticipate the next play as well as increase the efficacy of player movement on the court. It will also help shift your concentration from individual criticisms and statistics to a broader sense of team-oriented court awareness.

MODULE 2 : CONFIDENCE

"Confidence is where the training and the mindset intersect. If you put the time in, you can develop confidence."

Kevin Hambly, Stanford University Head Women's Volleyball Coach 2017 - present.

Confidence on the court is critical to the success of any volleyball player. It can make or break matches, seasons, and even careers. It is especially important for players in natural leadership positions, such as setters and liberos, to maintain confidence on the court so they can inspire others when things don't go as planned.

A variety of factors can threaten player confidence. A physical injury, position change, or a high-pressure match can all shake up confidence. If you're joining a new team or expected to play a starting role your first season in college, your self confidence is likely to be challenged. Sometimes a crisis of confidence can even stem from your own volleyball coach if they use the "old-school" coaching style of vocal intimidation and demeaning motivation.

Kathy Gregory, UC Santa Barbara's four-time AVCA West Region Coach of the Year and USBVA Hall of Fame member insisted that her players line up on the end line from shortest to tallest at the start of every practice. The players on her team called this activity "the firing squad" because that's what it felt like when Gregory would go down the line and one-by-one verbally rip us apart for our weaknesses, mistakes, stats, decisions, and sometimes even our personal lives. There was no topic that was considered out-of-bounds.

Nothing too personal or sacred for her excavation. She would badger her players about anything and everything. These sessions weren't always entirely negative, but rarely did we get through them without at least one player's confidence being damaged.

As a four-year player and Division I AVCA All-American for Coach Gregory at UCSB, I witnessed the confidence of my teammates fluctuate drastically over the course of a season. I myself experienced crises of confidence over the course of my career there. The good news is that low self-confidence is not a permanent state of being. Confidence is within your power to change. It can be developed, trained, and enhanced just like every other physical skill in volleyball.

Before I begin explaining how to build confidence in both players and teams alike, I think it's important to first define the term itself.

Confidence is a player's belief in their ability to reach a set result or established goal. It's what motivates players to take risks on the court, despite the fear of failing. In the world of volleyball, confidence equates to wanting the ball.

As a libero or back-row defensive player, it means being

aggressive in serve receive and on defense.

Confident hitters always want to get set regardless of who is blocking on the other side of the net, what happened on the previous play, or what the scoreboard says.

Confident setters are willing to take a chance on a low-percentage play during the match. They're not overly concerned about how to get the ball to the target or whose turn it is to swing. Instead they're looking across the net to read the block and communicating the plan of attack to their hitters. They use each player as a tool to intimidate, distract, and confuse their opponent in a calculated effort to dominate every point.

The biggest obstacle players need to overcome is fear. Fear of failure leads to self-doubt and apprehension. Doubting one's ability to accomplish a goal is dangerous in any endeavor but absolutely detrimental during competition. Confidence must come from within and there are ways of accessing, building, and strengthening it as a player develops.

So how do you build your confidence?

1. Let go of mistakes immediately.

Volleyball is a game of mistakes. Even at the highest level, there are no perfect games played. Often the winner is simply the team that makes the fewest errors.

You already know this. Yet, every single play we unreasonably expect perfection. We immediately assign a positive or negative value to each touch made on the ball and, more often than not, this is done before the play is even over.

Pass the ball on target without making the setter move…good.

Miss it to the left forcing the setter to the sideline eliminating an attacker… bad.

A quick set on tempo to the outside hitter splitting the opposing block…good.

A trap set with a double block on the right side…bad.

So what is the result of assigning judgment to every play?

In addition to distraction, it alters the state of confidence in your abilities.

If you are thinking about whether your last touch in a rally was good or bad then you're not thinking about the next play. You can't judge your last play and focus on what's coming next at the same time.

Self-awareness is a critical part of the learning process. Players need to be cognizant of the *causes* of mistakes in order to make the necessary adjustments in practices and in games. However, being aware of the cause of a mistake on the court and consciously letting go of it is very different than judging a mistake in and equating it to your self-worth on the court or ability as a player.

Do not allow those negative thoughts to infiltrate your mind. It does no good to punish yourself for a mistake by dwelling on it. Your destructive internal dialogue will transmit negative energy towards your teammates. Attitude is contagious on the court. One error can quickly turn into a pattern of errors if you don't let it go.

It's impossible to focus on the next play if you're still ruminating over the last one. The leading cause of mistakes in games is lack of focus. Reflection on past errors is the primary distractor. It's a vicious cycle. The best way to let go of mistakes immediately is to shift your attention towards preparing for the next play.

2. Negative thought replacement.

Negative self-talk is the primary source of low confidence on the court. When negative self-talk begins, muscles tighten. Your abilities to make decisions are impacted as they shift from being aggressive to being careful in order to avoid making mistakes. Excuses start to emerge and players naturally try to defend themselves by passing blame. This deflection can be directed at others on the court, coaches, or even outside sources such as distracting fans and overbearing parents.

It is human nature to be hardest on oneself and athletes often tend to be even more self-critical. Despite encouraging words from coaches or family members, there is a voice inside your head that only you can hear. It suggests an easier route and justifies quitting. As volleyball becomes more competitive, this incessant track of negative internal chatter is the reason so many young players give up the game.

At the age of only 14 years-old, Debbie Green wanted to quit the game of volleyball because she felt her coaches didn't want to coach her. At 5 foot 4 inches tall and weighing only 105 pounds, she was hardly a dominant presence on the court. She wasn't even able to consistently serve the ball over the net her freshman year in high school.

"My favorite two words were *I can't*", Green told a large group of aspiring setters at her annual setting camp in Long Beach, California in July, 2015. "My coach told me that if I worked really hard I might be able to make the varsity team by my junior year in high school. Instead, at 16, I was setting for the national team at the 1974 world championships in Mexico City."

What changed for the 14 year old freshman who couldn't serve the ball over the net?

It was her *mindset*.

Green made a conscious decision to commit to positive thinking. She replaced her "I can't" thoughts with "I can" and "I will". She dedicated herself to a grueling practice routine and made believing in her dreams a habit. She continues to inspire hundreds of coaches and young athletes today with her life story of perseverance and overcoming the negative self-talk that almost ended her career before it began.

In 1984, Green led her team to the podium winning a silver medal in the XXIII Olympiad in Los Angeles. At the time, it was the best finish in U.S. women's volleyball history.

The most powerful antidote for negative self-talk is *positive affirmation*. When negative thoughts start to creep into the minds of players and confidence begins to wane, reciting an inspirational mantra or shifting attention to long-term goals is an extremely effective technique to combat destructive thought patterns. Repetitively reminding yourself that you **can** and **will** achieve your goals can be extremely impactful. The key here is habitual dedication.

In order to redefine your internal narrative, you've got to re-write the script.

Here are three sample positive affirmations to say in the morning before you get out of bed, prior to stepping on the court, or during competition in between points. You can use these or create your own.

Memorize them. Tape them up in your locker. Write them on your kneepads. Type them into the notepad of your phone. Whatever works!

1. I love competition and perform my best under pressure.

2. No matter what happens on the court, I can do

this.

3. I am strong and I am powerful.

The two best times to reflect upon your positive affirmations are first thing in the morning, right after you get out of bed and before a match, right before you step foot onto the court. These are the times when athletes are most vulnerable and susceptible to insecurity, nervousness, and fear.

It is so easy to let self-doubt dominate your thoughts and it's natural to fear failing. You must reject the negative voice inside your head. You must silence the dangerous judgments and replace them with powerful declarations.

Everyday you have a choice to make. You can choose to take a conscious breath, grip tightly to your goals, and stand firm, or you can let the world tell you that you're not enough.

Find the right words that will speak to the deepest desires of your heart and choose to believe that you have the power to achieve them. Know that you have the ability to improve, overcome, and ultimately reach both your individual and team goals.

3. Approach competition with clear tactical plans.

Study the tendencies of your opponents. Know both their strengths and their weaknesses. With the advancement of video sharing and sports software tools like Data Volley, there is absolutely no excuse for being blindsided by players across the net. Before you step into the gym, you should already be familiar with the habits of your opposition and how to use them to your advantage. In the context of confidence building, identifying the tendencies and, more importantly, the weaknesses of your opponents is critical to maintaining a clear and focused objective.

When the match is on the line and the pressure mounts, players invariably resort to their tendencies. That go-to power shot or the favorite high percentage set. We've all experienced it on the court at one time or another.

Envision your team in this situation:

The opposing team is in rotation two (meaning their OH1 is in the left front position). The outsider hitter is 6'2" and touches 10'4". She's their most valuable player and your team is intimidated by her power on the court.

However by scouting and reviewing footage, you've learned that she hits angle almost exclusively and that she tips when the set is inside. So you tell your blockers to commit to blocking angle and give up the line entirely. You move your setter up to cover the tip.

Sure enough, a pass off the net results in a trap set to the anticipated outside hitter. She's got nowhere to go so she tips. Your setter is right there waiting.

Statistics matter. They have a way of shining a spotlight on what's lacking. Focusing your attention towards the weaknesses of opponents, rather than their strengths, can do wonders for the confidence of your team. The OH1 might be a force at the net and crush the angle, but knowing that her efficiency plummets when she attempts to hit the line or that she tips when the ball is set inside is critically valuable information.

It's human nature to compare your skill level to that of an opponent's and it's difficult not to immediately focus on things the competition can do that you cannot. By recognizing tendencies and targeting weaknesses of the team across the net, you'll feel like you have the mental advantage. To prevent self-doubt in games, shift your focus towards tactics. Knowing your opponents and developing a strategy to target their weaknesses is the key to winning points mentally when you're outmatched physically.

4. Train harder than anyone.

Train harder than your teammates. Train harder than your opponents. Train harder than everyone you know and anyone you've ever heard of. Hard work is an antidote to a crisis of confidence.

Hard work doesn't end when practice is over. To reach the next level, you've got to get extra repetitions outside of team training.

This may mean spending countless hours in solitude, passing, setting, and serving against a wall. This may mean picking up a new teammate and spending your off-season learning the beach game. It may require hiring a private trainer or attending a summer camp. It's your responsibility to improve through extra hours of practice and conditioning. There's simply not enough practice time for coaches to train each individual during standard team practices.

Because my father was an Olympic volleyball player, I had the privilege to get access to world-class volleyball role models and top-quality coaches. The legendary living room stories I grew up with, often included a reminder of the work it took to get there. Of all the volleyball legends I've met and stories I've heard over time, the character that most concretely depicts the perseverance, dedication, and work ethic of a lone volleyball player is that of Henry Bergman training by himself at East Beach.

Bergman is a name unknown to most people today, but he is still referred to by Karch Kiraly as one of the original trailblazers of beach volleyball. A silver plaque on the first men's court at East Beach in Santa Barbara honors Bergman's accomplishments as a famed beach volleyball player in the 1960's.

At a time when there was no prize money, no sponsors, and no Olympic medals for beach volleyball players, Bergman would train on the beach by himself everyday.

When the typical East Beach winds would rise up in the afternoon and the courts abandoned due to difficult playing conditions, Bergman would begin his training. With only one ball to his name, he would throw it up in the air and annihilate it. The ball would roll down the beach past the end line and on to the next court. He'd run to the ball and do it again. He would work his way down East Beach and all the way back up. Set after set and court after court. He did it in the toughest conditions when there was nobody else playing, training or watching. Without care of what anyone else thought, without the benefit of sponsorships or financial backing, and without any motivation of celebrity, Bergman trained himself to be the best volleyball player he could be.

The summer of 1968 witnessed Henry Bergman and Larry Rundle defeat Ron Lang and Ron Von Hagen in a seven-hour double elimination final of the Manhattan Beach Open- the most sought after beach volleyball title of the era. When the sun set on the beach that day, the men battled out the championship in darkness dimly lit from the headlights of parked cars. The championship match is still considered by many to be one of the greatest demonstrations of men's beach volleyball ever played.

When a player on a team out hustles everyone else in the gym, the impact is infectious. A single player can raise the standard and work ethic of an entire team. Morgan Hentz, a 5'9" defensive specialist, was that player for the Stanford Women's Volleyball team in 2016. When she joined the Stanford squad as an incoming freshman, she turned heads on the court by chasing down one ball after another. Previously an outside hitter for her club team, she was always expected to play the role of libero for the Cardinal.

In my interview with former Stanford Head Coach

John Dunning, he recounted Morgan's impact on the team his final year of coaching, "She went that hard every day of practice and every game. Even as a freshman, she had an amazing amount of emotional response in her if someone else didn't. You can imagine seniors who thought they were the hardest workers on a team and a freshman demanding of them to work harder. Everyone knew she was so invested and so committed to doing this. She works that hard at everything. I only coached her one season but I will forever be affected by her commitment".

Coach Dunning coached 32 years of college volleyball. He led 12 teams to the Final Four and won the National Championship 5 times. And yet, Morgan Hentz, just a freshman at the time, made a lasting impression on him with her exuberant confidence and work ethic.

Confidence is not something that anyone can develop for you. Don't expect confidence to come from an outside source. You have to earn your own confidence with hard work and repetition. Just like if you want to get an A in class, you need to study and invest the time into your craft. Confidence comes from the extra effort we invest in ourselves, the way we talk to ourselves and the way we carry ourselves on the court.

MODULE 3 : MINDSET

"Job number one for all of us, starting with me, starting with our staff, but also for all of our athletes, is to be learners and embrace the growth mindset. We have to be in a constant state of learning, creating a safe environment to do that and operate at the edge of our abilities and take risk."

Karch Kiraly, Two-time Olympic gold medalist in indoor and beach volleyball and U.S. Women's National Volleyball Team Head Coach.

Do you believe in your ability to improve this season? Do you believe in your team's ability to improve throughout the course of the season? Do your teammates believe?

If you're not sure, ask them. Ask them if they truly believe that your team can improve and achieve your team goals with commitment and dedication. Ask them if they truly believe you can achieve your season goals.

If you don't want to answer this question in front of your teammates, chances are *you* lack belief.

You may be happy with your jump serve or the way you play defense. You may be proud of your hitting percentage or how many kills you got in the last match. But if you don't truly believe that you and your teammates have the ability to improve and reach your team goals, then you won't. Disbelief among players can be crippling to the success of the team.

As a player and a team leader, it is critical to be conscious of the landscape of your team's mindset during practice and when entering into competition. Here's a 3-step game plan to change your mindset.

1. Adopt a growth mindset.

As a player, having belief in your ability to improve with practice is essential to developing and succeeding throughout your career. It is critical you trust in the potential of your ability to improve *and* your teammates ability to improve during the course of a season. A growth mindset believes that improvement is possible at every level.

In her book *Mindset: The New Psychology of Success*, Carol S. Dweck explains that, "in a growth mindset, people believe that their most basic abilities can be developed through dedication and hard work — brains and talent are just the starting point."

Here are a few key indicators of growth mindset in a player:

1. A growth mindset welcomes feedback and constructive criticism.

2. A growth mindset evaluates and learns from tough losses.

3. A growth mindset embraces obstacles and challenges as opportunities to learn and improve.

4. A growth mindset believes that you are more than

your mistakes on the court.

5. A growth mindset believes that you will improve over time and views practice as the path towards mastery.

A fixed mindset is the opposite of a growth mindset. Unwillingness to change habits, learn new skills or accept constructive criticism are all signs of a fixed mindset. A fixed mindset doesn't believe in your ability to evolve or improve as a player.

In the late 1960's and 1970's, Stan Gosciniak had been the Polish national team setter for over a decade. He was well known in the international volleyball world as a magician on the court and, during the peak of his career, the undisputed best setter in the world. He had a reputation for staring his opponents in the eye before his deceptive hands effortlessly floated the ball against the flow of the block.

After an impressive career of dominating the international platform and a stint playing in the International Volleyball Association (IVA), he spent years coaching the Polish men's national team. As a result of the friendships Stan fostered during his time playing in America with the IVA, he frequently returned to the US to coach elite level volleyball camps with Marv Dunphy each summer.

In his training sessions with teams, quantifiable improvement was always the goal. Stan would identify specific weaknesses in each player's skill set and chart their advancement in every practice.

If a player's chart indicated they were weak hitting down the line, then practice time would be dedicated to a drill in which the player would develop that specific skill. After completing the drill, results would be registered and improvement reflected in the appropriate area of his or her chart.

Each drill had a thoughtful purpose with a specific player or set of players in mind. The goal of every drill and every practice was to improve a specific skill set.

It was not about winning or losing. It was not about the starting lineup. It was about making each individual player better by the time they left the gym each day.

A lofty goal? Maybe. A tiring ambition? Definitely. But that was the objective of each of his training sessions. Over time, after the players bought into his philosophy, the improvement followed, as did the shift in perspective during practice and competition.

The process of improvement requires you to actually *believe* that you are getting better. If you don't believe you can improve, your performance in competition will reflect your disbelief.

As a player with a growth mindset, identifying your weaknesses is the key to improving throughout the course of a season. As a leader, it's your job to cultivate a culture of belief in the improvement potential of the team as a whole. The process of measuring and charting improvement can also be a powerful tool for developing a growth mindset on the court both individually and collectively.

When Kirsten Bernthal Booth took over the head coaching position at Creighton University in 2002, the team had a record of 3-23. Since 2012, the team has consistently been in the AVCA's Top 25 teams each year. In an interview with Coach Booth, I asked what her strategy was for transforming the culture of her program. Her strategy can be summed up in one word – process. "I've always been a coach that believes in process," Coach Booth shared, "doing the right things and not being totally locked into outcomes. To me, as an athlete and as a coach, that frees you a little bit. We really focus on process and taking risks."

Coach Booth explained that in her gym, if a player had a perfect set and tipped on game point, they could expect to get yelled at for making a low-risk decision. Conversely, if the hitter had a perfect set and they swung hard at it on game point, regardless of outcome, they were not going to be punished. Belief in the process has allowed players at Creighton University to take higher risks and continue to reach for their highest potential without fear of ramifications. This example demonstrates how an individual and team's adoption of a growth mindset can elevate the level of the team and the program over time if everyone trusts the process.

Most inexperienced volleyball players have a tendency to stop being aggressive under pressure and simply play it safe. When the game is on the line, they get tentative and shy away from shots that have been working for them the entire match. It's so easy to get influenced by the scoreboard. Game point can steal focus away from the true objective. It's important to remember that you cannot measure player or team progress by the win-loss record or statistics alone.

One of the keys to performing better under pressure is shifting player focus from *results* to *improvement*. By changing your mindset and concentrating on getting better every touch, you will also gain confidence in your abilities.

Another key factor to developing a growth mindset is your willingness to learn new skills. For some of you, that might even mean learning to play a new position all-together. It is very common for players to change positions between the transition from high-school to college.

When Misty May-Treanor arrived at Long Beach State for her first day of practice, Brian Gimmillaro told her that she was going to be their setter. After having led her Newport Harbor High School team to the State Championship as an outside hitter, she was expected to not only start over at a new position but also play a leading role as a freshman for one of the best collegiate teams in the country. Debbie Green, the Long Beach State assistant coach at the time, was tasked with teaching her how to set.

Misty tells this story to all the aspiring young setters at her *Dreaming In Gold* volleyball camp as an example of one the most challenging obstacles she was forced to overcome throughout her career. Misty recognized that if she was going to get the playing time she wanted her freshman year, she needed to develop entirely new skills and learn how to be a setter.

As a young player, Misty chose to commit herself

entirely to the training regiment put forth by Long Beach State. By continuing to expand her skill set and adapt to learning a different position on the court, Misty classically modeled and embraced the growth mindset.

The training paid off. The 1998 Long Beach State team that Misty captained her senior year was the first women's NCAA volleyball team to have an undefeated season and Misty was elected AVCA player of the year in both 1997 and 1998. Certainly the setting skills she developed in college contributed to her illustrious beach career to follow.

In this book, I'm not going to cover training technique. I'm simply emphasizing the importance of believing that your fundamental skills can be improved through perseverance. In my conversations with elite volleyball players and coaches at every level, I have heard this simple advice echoed again and again.

2. Change your court vocabulary.

While speaking with John Kessel, the Director of Sport Development for USA Volleyball, I pressed him for advice on how to mentally train players. For decades Kessel has taught the game of volleyball to players around the globe. He's a seasoned veteran player, coach and lifelong student of the sport.

Without hesitation, his advice was to change the court vocabulary of players. The key, he insisted, is to eliminate these four words: try, don't, but and can't.

Let's start by explaining the consequences of the word *try*. "When I let the word *try* come into my gym, then I'm giving the athlete an excuse to *not* do something", Kessel explained.

It helps to think about it in terms outside of volleyball. For instance, take an invitation to a party of which the date conflicts with a previous commitment. In a passing conversation with the host, the words, "I'll *try* to make it to your party tomorrow night" come out of your mouth before you even have time to cross check your schedule. The presence of *try* signifies non-commitment. Maybe but maybe not. By adding the word try you've given yourself an excuse to not attend. Based upon your response, the host won't be surprised by your absence.

Now let's apply it to volleyball. The instructions to the setter are, "try to set the middle on the next play". The *try* gives her the justifiable excuse she needs to go outside if the pass is uncomfortably far off the net. Or consider this directive to the server, "try not to serve the libero". Try is the grace stipulation that creates a large margin for error.

Instead of telling your middle that you're going to *try* to set them on the next play, give her a specific set of instructions depending on the location of the pass and lineup of the opposing offense. Or better yet, encourage her to get up early and give you a vocal target regardless of where the pass is.

Moving on to Kessel's bad word number two - *don't*. The undesirable consequences of this word are self-evident. Think about what immediately comes to your mind when somebody says, "don't serve the ball in the net". The result is that the mind envisions the volleyball net. Or worse, a ball landing in the net. When you picture yourself serving the ball into the net, the mind doesn't differentiate between a positive and negative. Therefore it's damaging to direct your thoughts to envision the exact action that you want to avoid.

Bad word number three … *but*. I was going to hit down the line, but I saw the block and decided to tip instead. I was going to set the middle, but she was late therefore I had to go outside again. I was going to serve zone 4 but the libero pushed the outside hitter up near the net to cover the shorty.

You see the pattern yet? The *but* cancels the intention of whatever action precedes it in the sentence. It's ok to make adjustments during the play in reaction to reading the opponent. In fact, all the best players do. Rather than giving an excuse for not implementing the desired play, try voicing with confidence the strategy behind your conviction to calling an audible.

Eliminate the *but* and commit to the flow of the play. Be cognizant and direct about the reason behind every change in decision. Analyze and honestly discuss the consequences. Eliminating the *but* will strengthen your position as a mental leader on the court, and create trust among your teammates.

And finally, the worst four letter word of every gym… *can't*. When negative self talk turns into negative court conversation, it's detrimental to yourself and your teammates. It also fuels the confidence of the opposition when they see a player or team beginning to doubt their own ability. The word *can't* unravels confidence, momentum and even team chemistry. Drop the apostrophe 't'. Change your mindset towards a journey of improvement. You can and you will. If not today, then someday soon. Maybe even the next attempt.

There are no negative consequences to eliminating this verbiage. These four little words might seem harmless but they have no place on the volleyball court. Removing them from your internal and external dialogue will make a big impact on your perspective. Changing the way you speak is the first step in transforming your mindset.

3. Always compete.

Always compete in practice and in conditioning drills. Compete in every rally of every game regardless of what the scoreboard says. Compete against your opponents. And most importantly, compete against the player you were when you began that day.

In today's world, college scholarships and starting positions are always on the line. The game has added levels of pressure and as a result some of the purity of competition has been lost. Results have real impacts on the lives of players and as well as their families. It's so easy to let the goal of a college scholarship eclipse the team's pursuit of improvement and victory. It's often tempting for collegiate players to rank AVCA All-American Honors above the "big dance" at the end of every season. We've got to fight to retain the authenticity of the game and the purity of competition.

As a player, you should compete against yourself and your teammates every opportunity you get, whether it be during practice drills or a match with the season on the line. You've got to earn your right to play on the court. Sometimes, you've even got to ask for an opportunity to prove yourself.

Courtney Thompson is the first to admit that one of her biggest challenges on the volleyball court is being short. Standing at only 5'7", many people throughout her career told her she should be a libero, insisting that she'd never make it as a setter at the next level.

In 2005, she led the University of Washington to a NCAA Division 1 Women's Volleyball Championship title over the favored Nebraska in a shocking 3-0 victory. A fairytale story for those that favor the under-sized-dog, but Courtney's ambition didn't end there.

After the completion of her final college season, she actually called the USA volleyball committee and asked for permission to tryout as a setter. A bold move given her height and the 2012 Olympic games around the corner. The battle to make the national team roster was fiercely competitive. Courtney's hard work and perseverance was rewarded with a spot on the 2012

Olympic team that won the silver medal in London. The 2012 Olympics was just the beginning of her illustrious professional career as a setter dominating the international scene. Now as a bronze medalist at the 2016 Olympic Games and a silver medalist at the 2012 Olympic Games, there are few coaches that would limit her playing time or cut her from the team.

What if Courtney hadn't made that life altering phone call asking for permission to compete for a spot on the team?

In 2016 the University of Stanford women's volleyball team was the 11th seed going into the NCAA tournament. In the quarter final match Stanford drew the 3rd seed – the University of Wisconsin at Wisconsin. In an arena filled with nearly 7,000 Wisconsin fans cheering against them, the Stanford women found themselves down 2-0 with four starting freshmen on the floor. In the locker room between games 2 and 3, Inky Ajanaku – Stanford's 6'3" middle blocker, stepped into a new zone.

In an interview with me, Coach John Dunning recalled Inky's game-changing speech to her team, "You've been listening to people say we're too young to win and you're wrong. I'm with you every day and I know that's not the case. You just have the ability to do something no one else has ever done. And so we are going to go do that." The Stanford women returned to the court and won the next 3 consecutive sets. Then they went on to win the Final Four in Columbus, Ohio. Coach Dunning believes Inky influenced that sequence of events with much more than just her playing ability, it was her character, determination and belief that altered the course of her team's destiny that year.

Competitiveness is contagious. It's especially contagious among teammates working towards a common goal. When you make a commitment to competing in practice, you're mentally preparing yourself to compete in competition under pressure.

MODULE 4 : THE ZONE

"You can't think and hit at the same time."

Yogi Berra, Professional baseball player and 10-time World Series Champion.

When I watch the best players in the world play volleyball, there is one thing that always surprises me.

Sure, at that level, they can all hammer the ball. Their passing is usually flawless. The sets are consistently on target and very difficult to read. Their footwork on defense is so efficient that it appears they're barely moving and yet somehow covering the entire court at the same time. And they all crush their serves.

I expect those common traits from the best volleyball players in the world. What amazes me the most is how they make it look so *effortless*.

They glide between positions, from defense to offense and back again with an almost precognitive notion of where the next touch will land. With no apparent urgency or stress, they seem to be not trying very hard and yet giving it their all at the same time.

Doug Beal, former USA Volleyball CEO noticed this pattern too. He says, "Good players rarely look like the game is stressful for them, and they never seem rushed because they adjust their position all the time based on what's happening. They're always compensating for the movement of their teammates and the movement on the other side of the court, whether it's blocking or back court[7]."

When the stakes are high and the pressure is on at the end of the game, do you think these players are thinking about the weight transfer in their footwork or the angle of their elbow in their arm swing?

Absolutely not.

They operate in a state of relaxed concentration with a focus dial directed on the next play. Their bodies produce the desired outcome without over-thinking the exact subset of physical movements necessary to produce the desired action.

In 1964, famed psychologist Abraham Maslow originally coined the term "peak experience[8]" to describe these periods of heightened concentration and self-actualization. A few decades later the University of Chicago psychologist Mihaly Csikszentmihalyi coined the term "flow" to describe this state of optimal performance and intense focus in the present moment.

Today this rare and exhilarating altered state of consciousness in athletes is most commonly referred to as "peak performance" or "playing in the zone". You most often see it when athletes are under immense pressure and rise to the occasion by going far beyond their regular performance standards. Many athletes who have won national championships and Olympic gold medals attribute their enhanced performance to flow or playing in the zone.

The million dollar question that everyone wants to know the answer to is, how can you access the zone under pressure and allow yourself to play in the flow?

Unfortunately, there's no easy answer to that. Accessing the zone is still mostly a mystery. Players who have personally experienced playing in the zone often have difficulty replicating the experience. However, I do have four techniques that will clear your mind, relax your body and improve your focus in preparation for competition. You will find these strategies make a massive impact on your performance if practiced consistently.

1. Establish a dedicated pre-game routine.

The mind is not a switch that you can simply turn on and off. It is unreasonable to expect yourself to be able to immediately change gears the second you step foot on the court. Just as you transition from socializing or studying to sleep by winding down at night, you need time to shift your focus and block out distracting thoughts in preparation to play. To achieve peak performance, you need to prepare yourself mentally, emotionally and physically for competition.

Establishing a pre-game routine that works for you is essential to reach your full potential.

In my interview with Kevin Hambly, the head women's volleyball coach at Stanford University, he explains that an effective pre-game routine should include two key elements: an intentional individual activity done in solitude to center the self and an intentional group activity that brings the team together. The purpose is to get your mind ready to play your best and connect with your teammates before stepping on the court.

The best pre-game routine is individualized to suit the needs of each player. For some players, it might mean shutting off your phone, turning down the lights, focusing on your breath and guiding yourself through a meditation. For another player it might mean cranking up the music and having a goofy dance party in the locker room to relax.

Every player has unique needs and there should be no judgement around differences in pre-game routines. There is no right or wrong way to prepare. What you do for your pre-game routine doesn't matter as long as you do it consistently and with intention.

During my 2020 interview with Coach Hambly, he shared a story about the importance of Stanford's pre-game routine. Before a mid-season match-up between Stanford and the University of Kentucky, Stanford's typical pre-game routine was unintentionally cut short. The Stanford team bus arrived late to the gym, resulting in significantly less time for the players to prepare for the match. For this particular Stanford squad, taking 5-10 minutes to meditate and visualize before each match was something the players identified as a critical component to their preparation. But on this day, there was no time for it.

"We got absolutely smashed in the first set," said Coach Hambly "The score was like 25-14. Their breathing was off. Everything was off. You could just tell they were so anxious. So instead of saying anything or doing anything in the timeout, we literally meditated for those 3 minutes in the middle of the match. I told everyone to be quiet, go sit down or stand up, or do whatever to get your heads right and just breathe or meditate. We were a totally different team after that and we smashed them."

It is much easier to identify examples of the negative impacts of an interrupted pre-game routine than it is to spot the benefits of a consistent one. The benefits of your pre-game pattern may be subtle. It's common to overlook their impact on your physical performance when you're starting out. However, if you stay committed to the process, the benefits will build gradually over time.

2. Practice mindfulness.

The practice of meditation and the concept of mindfulness has its roots in Eastern spiritual traditions and is particularly central to Buddhism. However in the West, mindfulness and the practice of being present has become secularized as a widely accepted strategy to improve concentration, lower levels of anxiety, reduce stress and heighten awareness. My favorite definition of mindfulness is also one of the most simple. It comes from the American Psychological Association, "a moment-to-moment awareness of one's experience without judgment[9]".

A pre-game mindfulness exercise is a very effective strategy for players and teams to mentally warm-up before physically warming-up. Several top collegiate women's volleyball programs including Stanford University and Creighton University use mindfulness exercises as a way to center and focus their teams. Incorporating a dedicated pre-game ritual could be as simple as three to five minutes in a quiet place outdoors or in the locker room prior to ball handling.

When you are starting out with these mindfulness exercises, it is best to set yourself up for success by doing it in a location that is quiet and free from interruptions of any kind. This dedicated time is intended to eliminate distractions.

As you become more comfortable with the techniques, you can progressively relocate your practice to more exposed areas with greater distraction such as a loud locker room or eventually even the sidelines of the volleyball court.

Here's a sample pre-game mindfulness exercise to help you mentally transition from day-to-day life to a competitive environment. The following exercise should be done for a set period of time. It includes two different types of breathing techniques for you to try out. It's really important that you silent your cell phone during this practice, but you can set a timer on your phone to pull yourself out of the exercise so you're not worried about tracking time.

I. Sit in a comfortable seated position to cultivate self-awareness and release tension. (1 minute)

Close your eyes. Straighten your spine and relax all your major muscle groups. Scan your body for any areas of tension or discomfort. Don't pull away from the discomfort. Instead, lean into it. Breathe into it. Relax into it. What does your body feel like today?

Don't judge it, just notice it. Notice if one arm or leg is tighter than the other. Become aware of which body parts are in contact with outside surfaces such as a chair or the floor. The goal here is to become completely aware of your body positioning.

Pay attention to what's happening in the moment. Take in the sounds of your surroundings.

Start to relax the muscles in your jaw, neck, and shoulders. Wiggle your fingers. Curl your toes.

Now stop moving.

When it is time to be still, you might suddenly notice that you want to do something like fix your hair or adjust your shirt. Refrain from making adjustments. Don't itch the itch. But notice your habit of wanting to make adjustments when you're asked to remain still. If you can break that habit, then you can break any habit.

Accept the feelings of discomfort instead. Breathe into the discomfort. Laugh at your impatience. And then let go of those thoughts.

Remember, you don't need to worry about the time

because you've set your timer for 5 minutes.

II. Reset your breath with box breathing. (2 minutes)

Become aware of your breath pattern. Start by simply noticing whether you are breathing through your nose or your mouth.

When you're ready, experiment with controlling the depth of your inhale and the speed of your exhale by using the "box breathing method." The box breathing method has the following four parts[10]:

    1. breath in through your nose while counting to four slowly,

    2. then hold your breath deep inside your lungs for a count of four,

    3. next exhale your breath completely while you slowly count to four,

    4. and finally hold your exhale for a four count.

Repeat the box breath technique for approximately two minutes. If counting to four feels too hard, then reduce the count to three. If it feels too easy, increase the count to five or six. The purpose of this experience is to even out your breath and return your body to its natural rhythm. Follow your breath as a road map out of your head and into your body.

Feel your breath move up the front of your body and back down the back of your spine. Choose to stabilize yourself with your breath. You should be able to feel your body move with your breath. Recognize in yourself where your body needs more stability. Recognize in yourself where your body needs more spaciousness. Remember that you have the ability to regulate your breath at any time.

III. Concentrate on a focal point and let go. (2 minutes)

Now change your pattern to breathing in through your nose and exhaling through your mouth. This time when you inhale, think of the word "let" and when you exhale think of the word "go". Continuing thinking "let" on your inhale and "go" on your exhale. Continue breathing at your own pace for the remaining two minutes.

As you inhale, shrug your shoulders up to your ears and as you exhale, draw your shoulders down.

We'll do that again, draw your shoulders up and as you exhale release your shoulders down.

One more time, shrug your shoulders up to your ears and as you exhale let go and relax your shoulders.

Don't punish yourself when your mind starts to drift or if negative thoughts creep in. Just cultivate an awareness of your thought patterns during this exercise. Always gently bring your attention back to breath.

3. Create your own visualization script.

Visualization is another very effective technique for volleyball mindset training. The term visualization means, "the process of creating a mental image or intention of what you want to happen or feel in reality.[11]"

Visualization is often referred to as "mental rehearsal" or "guided imagery". The aim of visualization is to train your mind and body to feel calm under pressure situations and influence the outcome of events.

A visualization script is the story you tell yourself when you're rehearsing. Writing your own, personalized visualization script to prepare for high pressure matches is extremely powerful. A quality visualization script should identify who, where, when, and what. Who are you playing with and who are you playing against? Where are you playing (home or away)? When are you playing (morning, afternoon, night)? And what is the skill or play that you are rehearsing?

When visualizing yourself in action, it's picture-perfect form and the successful execution of a play that we're after. This can be done by replaying past successful actions or envisioning movements on the court you've practiced and hope to someday master.

Here's a sample visualization script for a volleyball match. Envision yourself as a player in a game and try rehearsing this scenario with me in your mind now.

Picture yourself walking into the locker room. You put on your volleyball jersey and knee pads. You lace up your shoes. You go through both your individual and team pre-game routines (from section 1 above). You feel calm and focused. You had a great week of practice and are well prepared for this match. You know that from the time you leave the locker to the time you start play is 45 minutes.

Now imagine yourself entering the gym, you scan the scene. You notice the color of the volleyball court and the lines on the floor. You take note of the ceiling height and location of the scoreboard. You notice the distance between the end of the service line and first row of the bleachers where the fans sit. In the background you hear the sound of both teams starting to warm up their arms – balls are bouncing, players are calling the ball, and volleyball shoes are squeaking on the floor. Both teams go through serve and pass, hitting lines and serving. The referee blows the whistle and calls for the floor captains. The coin toss ensues. It's determined that your team will start serving in rotation 1.

As the match starts, you feel strong and fresh. You feel quick on your feet and you're jumping high. Now take your attention across the net and zero in on the specific opponent that you are matched up against. Notice her arm-swing, whether she drops her elbow when she's about to tip or over-rotates her shoulders when she's preparing to swing down the line. Be conscious of what rotation the opposing team is in and whether or not the setter is in the front row.

Now slowly zoom in on a moment at the end of the match. Notice the number of time-outs left and the number of substitutions remaining. Your team is up by 1 and you've got an opportunity to win the match on this serve receive rotation. The opponent serves the ball to zone 5 right at you. You identify the direction of the serve early, adjust your footwork and platform to make a perfect on-target pass.

Then you reposition yourself to attack and callout to your setter with confidence to set you the ball on match point. The setter puts up a perfect set to you on the outside. The sound of the fans and your coaches fade away. You are completely focused on the ball now. As you make your approach time slows down. You take in where the defenders are on the other side. You can clearly see the whole in the block across the net. You reach, snap and hammer the ball down right between the block winning the match for your team.

You immediately look up at the scoreboard to confirm it's over. Your team rushes toward you. You suddenly hear the roar of the crowd. The feelings of excitement surge. You have succeeded in putting the ball away on game point during a high pressure situation.

Visualization before and during competition is a powerful mental training tool for all levels of volleyball players. It can be incorporated into pre-practice or pre-game rituals but it can also be utilized during competition, time outs, and even the short breaks between points.

It's important to recognize that some players are more visual than others. If you're a player who has trouble visualizing, then make a highlight real of yourself successfully executing a specific skill or defending an upcoming opponent. Kirsten Bernthal Boothe, the head coach of Creighton University Women's

Volleyball team, told me in a 2020 interview that their program utilizes this technique to build up player confidence.

Visualization, like any other skill, takes discipline and commitment. It's also critical to note that visualization works both ways; therefore it can actually be damaging if a player visualizes herself incorrectly or unsuccessfully executing a skill.

Visualization is most effective when a player is relaxed and in a safe place. It also helps to establish a fixed amount of time so that she is not preoccupied with the length of the exercise.

There's no excuse to neglect this valuable training tool. No gym is needed. Players don't need a net, a teammate, or even a ball. You just have to close your eyes and picture yourself executing the desired skills. It's easy to underestimate the power of these *mental reps* however, there's a reason why many of the best athletes in the world incorporate visualization into their training routines.

4. Get out of your head and into your body.

When Misty May-Treanor was learning the ropes as a

setter during her early years at Long Beach State, she naturally experienced confidence battles. Before one memorable high-pressure match, she found herself struggling in the warm-up. Debbie Green, her assistant coach at the time, took Misty aside and directed her to the locker room. Green pulled out a piece of paper and a pen. She told Misty to sign her signature on the paper. After Misty naturally signed her name, Green instructed her to replicate the signature precisely by staring at the original version and reproducing the exact curve of each letter. The result was two recognizably different signatures. Green then turned the paper over and told Misty to close her eyes and sign her name again. The blind signature perfectly matched the original version.

In this simple exercise, Green's demonstrated to Misty the consequences of overthinking and the importance of trusting her body. During a *Dreaming in Gold* volleyball camp, Misty recounted how this locker room handwriting experiment. When you feel yourself overthinking technique, sometimes the most effective strategy is to relax, focus on the present moment and trust your body. Once you've learned and practiced the fundamental skills of volleyball such as setting or hitting, you will be able to produce the desired movements under pressure if you trust your intuition and natural reaction.

Experienced players don't need to think about exact footwork or proper technique to hit or set a ball. They can do it from muscle memory and by a practiced and reproduced set of specific actions. They may not even be able to explain the steps of the skill but they can easily show how it's done.

Conversely, if the mind is overly focused on one single aspect of a technique, such as whether the right foot is forward instead of the left, then it will negatively influence the player's ability to achieve the desired result. If you're overly focused on footwork instead of the movement of the ball, then you will consequently lose sight of the objective. If relaxed concentration with focus directed on the next play is how we operate, then overloading your mind with technical information during competition detracts from the ultimate goal.

MODULE 5 : TEAMWORK

"Volleyball is one of the most interactive games going. It is a game of intuition, imagination, improvisation - but most of all, of reciprocity. Of teamwork. There is no way to freelance in volleyball.[12]"

MARV DUNPHY - USA Men's National Team Olympic Gold Medal Coach. Coached Pepperdine men's volleyball team to 5 NCAA titles

The most fundamental part of the mental game of volleyball is teamwork. Coaches frequently talk about the importance of teamwork in sideline huddles and dedicate time during pre-season to team-building exercises. Club coaches and recruiting directors often get asked by college coaches if a player being considered for a scholarship is a "good team player." And yet, despite the widely held belief that teamwork is a critical component to every successful season, few teams have clear strategies to unify a group of individual players into a cohesive team.

To get started, I think it's best to learn from legendary UCLA basketball coach John Wooden. In Coach Wooden's – *Pyramid of Success*[13] he identifies "team spirit" as a key building block to the livelihood of every team. Wooden describes team spirit as, "an eagerness to sacrifice personal interests of glory for the welfare of all." In Coach Wooden's recipe for team spirit, the word "sacrifice" is critical. He emphasizes the importance of sacrificing one's ego for the greater good of the group while striving toward a shared achievement. Cultivating a culture of teamwork is a shift in perspective from "me" to "us" that requires self-sacrifice.

When a group of individuals can click or unite together

under pressure, the momentum and feeling of invincibility can stretch the potential of the entire team. There is a sense of magic to the experience. In this way, I like to think of teamwork as a spiritual practice. I don't mean spiritual in the religious sense like Christianity or Buddhism. By spiritual I mean an intangible force that connects us to one another. It can be felt but not seen.

It's what feeds your energy after a big play. It's why momentum is contagious. It's what happens when teams go on scoring streaks and make big comebacks. It's the reason why some plays seem to be worth so much more than others despite only one point being earned. Momentum shifts around big plays at pivotal moments: a solo block, a long rally that ends in a definitive kill, or a seemingly impossible dig that quickly transitions into a point for the defensive team. These types of rallies carry an emotional weight. There is a palpable energy shift when the ball finally hits the floor.

Caren Kemner, 1992 Olympic bronze medalist, knows exactly what I'm talking about. Kemner says, "Once you get the taste of ruining somebody's great hit, it stays with you. And it changes the game. A great defensive play is worth about five points in emotion.[14]" The build up of emotion can take over matches. It's impossible to measure but it can be the difference between a win and loss.

When teams enter into this flow and feel emotionally connected, they seem to develop a single consciousness. It can feel as though you can communicate to your teammates with your eyes and read one another's minds. The physical movements of players seem synchronized. The trust between players on the court is so strong that the collective confidence of the team soars.

Pete Carroll, the head football coach of the NFL's Seattle Seahawks, captures the experience perfectly in his book entitled, *Win Forever – Live, Work, and Play Like a Champion*. Coach Carroll says that, "When a team can get into that state, the resulting acceleration and sense of invincibility allows them to reach a potential they never would have dreamed of as individuals. It's as if the team shared one heartbeat."

When a team can get into that mental state together, the feeling of invincibility among players is contagious. These mountain top moments are incredibly exhilarating when they happen to players individually, but when an entire team clicks together to experience it collectively everyone reaches unrealized success.

So how do you unite a team of individuals under pressure? What does a healthy culture of teamwork look like on the court? How do we break down the emotional barriers between teammates that impact performance?

Let's take a look at five (5) key practices to implement on your team.

1. Shift your worldview from scarcity to abundance.

Competition among teammates is a natural part of the game. From the moment you step foot into the gym, it can feel as though you are competing against both your teammates and your opponents. Every player is competing for a starting spot on the team. And when there aren't enough starting spots on the court to go around, teamwork doesn't always come naturally.

Competition among teammates in practices and scrimmages can expose weaknesses and motivate players to train harder, however it can also propagate a destructive worldview of scarcity among players. A worldview of scarcity may sound like a lofty concept for volleyball players, but it is present at the foundation of every team struggle regardless of age or ability. Let me explain.

A worldview of scarcity is a belief or feeling that there is not enough of _____ (fill in the blank) to go around. It's a power struggle between teammates driven by ego rather than improvement. We all know this feeling. There are only 6 starting spots on the team. There isn't enough playing time. There's a shortage of scholarships available. You didn't get enough sets in the game. Only one player on the team gets voted Most Valuable Player. There's not enough accolades, credit or power to be shared among the team. It's a selfish win or lose mentality that postures teammates against one another. A worldview of scarcity feeds resentment among teammates and attacks self-confidence. It's a perspective that prioritizes personal stats and awards over the team's collective success.

A worldview of abundance is the opposite of scarcity. A worldview of abundance prioritizes the team's victory over individual statistics. Here teammates rush towards each other in celebration to share high-fives and fist pumps. Rather than obsessing over your mistakes or amount of playing time, celebrate the accomplishments of all your teammates. Everyone's contribution on the court is recognized and equally valued. The on target pass. The deceptive set. The middle blocker's fake attack to draw in opposing blockers. The tight defensive coverage surrounding the outside hitter as she swings for a critical point. These are all critical components of successful playmaking. Without the pass or set, the attacker wouldn't be able to take a swing. Players with a worldview of abundance are quick to point out the contributions of their teammates and celebrate the success of their teammates.

Competition in sports inherently cultivates a win or loss worldview of scarcity. And yet, the best players, teammates and leaders in the world understand that the competition is really only with yourself, not your teammates.

Nobody understands this better than U.S Soccer Olympic Gold Medalist Abby Wambach. As the world record holder for international goals for both female and male soccer players, and co-captain of the 2015 World Cup Champion Team, Abby sidelined herself in the last World Cup of her career because she knew that as one of the oldest players on the team, she no longer was the best option for her starting position. In her recent book Wolfpack, Abby explains, "Championing each other can be difficult for women because for so long we have been pitted against each other for the token seat at the table. Maintaining the illusion of scarcity is how power keeps women competing for the singular seat at the old table, instead of uniting and building a new, bigger table.[15]" Teamwork is not a power hierarchy. The greatest teammates don't grab at power, instead they share it.

In a podcast interview with WiSP Sports in 2019, Heather Olmstead, the Head Women's volleyball coach at Brigham Young University echoed this philosophy. Reflecting upon her team's Final Four finish of the previous season, Coach Olmstead had this to say about her program, "We want to create opportunities for young women to compete and teach them that it's okay to be competitive, and teach them that it's okay to want something for yourself, but we also need to be able to meld that with the team, what's best for the team and how that helps the team goals. But we also want to teach them that in the end the competition is really just with yourself and not with your teammates or even the team across the net. Our quest here at BYU is to see how good *you* can be.[16]"

When you truly believe that everyone on the team contributed to the win, there's always enough credit to be shared. A worldview of abundance doesn't always come naturally to teams, but it can be curated over time. The power and joy of collective triumph always overcomes tension between individual teammates.

2. Make a pledge to not gossip about teammates.

Gossiping is lethal among teams. A culture of team gossiping will fracture friendships, shatter trust between teammates and rapidly dissolve confidence among players. Over the course of an entire season, gossip has the power to destroy the very foundation of teamwork as a whole.

Recent medical studies documented in the Harvard Business Review actually document evidence of diminishing collaboration among teams that display incivility towards one another. Christine Porath, an Associate Professor at the McDonough School of Business at Georgetown University, writes that "Incivility can fracture a team, destroying collaboration, splintering members' sense of psychological safety, and hampering team effectiveness. Belittling and demeaning comments, insults, backbiting, and other rude behavior can deflate confidence, sink trust, and erode helpfulness — even for those who aren't the target of these behaviors.[17]"

And yet, gossip occurs so regularly among teams that most players don't even realize when they're doing it! Just think back to your past experiences on teams. Have you ever been hurt by the words from a teammate that weren't intended for you to overhear?

I've personally witnessed the destructive power of poisonous gossip on many teams. I also regretfully caused pain with my words in the past and I've been hurt by the words of others. Overhearing your teammates talk negatively about you behind your back feels absolutely devastating. It's hard to recover from. In some cases, it can even be impossible to rebuild the friendship.

The best solution is pledging as a team to not gossip about teammates.

Establishing a simple, yet powerful, no gossiping policy on your team can make a big impact on how teammates develop trust in one another throughout the season. The pledge should contain at least these two (2) key components;

6. I pledge to not talk about teammates when they are absent.

7. I pledge to speak up and intervene if I overhear harmful gossiping about my teammates.

Making a vow to hold teammates accountable is just as important as refraining from gossip yourself. It's important to recognize that when it comes to team gossip, individual silence is often viewed as a form of consent. Just as witnesses to bullying are considered bystanders. Often victims of hurtful gossip feel more alone because witnesses don't take any form of action to stop the abuse. Therefore when you overhear members of your team talking negatively about a teammate, it's your responsibility to stop the destructive behavior by standing up for the victim being targeted. Accountability is key to creating a team culture without gossip.

For the team pledge to be successful, players must be willing to hold one another accountable and be held accountable. It works both ways. Breaking a habit of gossip is not an easy task. From reality television shows to social media feeds, gossip is so common in our culture. Changing the pattern starts with awareness. Begin by becoming mindful of your own words and the feelings they stir up. Notice how speaking negatively about somebody triggers feelings. Does gossiping make you feel empowered? Or does it make you feel a little sad afterwards? Maybe you even feel a twinge of guilt. These are all important feelings to pay attention to. Developing consciousness is the key.

The reality is that we often underestimate the degree of

damage caused by negative words. The consequences of hurtful gossiping can extend far beyond the boundaries of the volleyball court. Gossiping is the most common and understated form of bullying. According to studies by Yale University, students that are bullied are 2 to 9 times more likely to consider suicide than non-victims[18]. Harmful language can actually cost lives. Alternatively loyal teammates can become life saving allies.

Pledging as a team to not gossip about teammates leads to deeper trust between teammates and higher confidence among teams as a whole. This simple team pledge is such a powerful practice, but you'll find it's difficult to follow. I encourage you to stay committed to the pledge. Make it part of your team's core values. Display the pledge visibly in your team locker room or gym. Banning gossip is a critical step to building a safe and supportive team environment.

Obviously not all conflicts within teams stem from gossip, therefore having a strategy to resolve conflicts between players on and off the court can be extremely helpful for teams. The first best step is always to try directly speaking to the person that you have a problem with. Most team conflicts can be resolved by giving the other player an opportunity to explain, or apologize.

However, if the negative or harmful behavior continues, then asking a team leader to step in is the best next step. Oftentimes, getting a third perspective from a neutral player will solve the problem. The last resort for team conflict resolution is seeking involvement from a member of the coaching staff.

3. Develop systems of communication.

Under pressure, team's often experience a breakdown in communication on the court. Many high-stakes games are lost because of a lack of communication between players on the court. When a game or season is on the line some players tend to get more vocal, while others quiet down. What most players don't realize is that communication is a skill that must be developed, just like passing or setting. You can't expect to communicate with your teammates well under the pressure of a match if you haven't developed a system of communication.

In his book *Beyond Basketball,* Mike Krzyzewski (more commonly known as "Coach K") refers to a different language that players speak during a game. "On the basketball court", Coach K says, "there is very little time to get your message across. In the heat of a game, a basketball team speaks a different language; it is not a language based on long sentences, but it is a language nonetheless. To acclimate our team to speaking this language, we do not merely drill defensive stances and positioning in our practices, we drill talking. When you talk, your body reacts, your hands get ready, and your mind becomes prepared to respond, even under pressure.[19]" Communication, Coach K says, prepares both your mind and body to perform. To unite a team under pressure, court language must be learned and rehearsed.

Basically, we've got to establish how to effectively communicate with each other both on and off the court. The three most important components of communication among teammates are to communicate concisely, listen and provide acknowledgement. Lots of people are good at talking, but fewer players listen well. To be a good communicator, you've got to do both in addition to acknowledging comprehension. If you don't acknowledge that you heard your teammate or coach, then they will doubt whether or not you heard or understood them. The acknowledging piece is often overlooked among players. One of the best steps you can take to improve your communication with teammates and coaches is make a commitment to always acknowledge them both on and off the court. On the court it can be as simple as making eye-contact with the person and saying, "got it!" Off the court, it means always replying to emails and text-messages.

Between-play Communication vs During-play Communication

When trying to improve team communication, it is also important to differentiate between types of communication on the court. Between-play communication is the dialogue between players and coaches when the ball is not in motion. This takes place in the team huddle between serves and during time-outs. During-play communication is the language that players use to convey messages to their teammates in the middle of a rally when the ball is in play.

There is a big difference between the two types of communication. When pressure builds in a match, most teams have unproductive between-play chatter and experience a breakdown in during-play communication.

Oftentimes between-play communication sounds more like cheerleading. It's well intentioned but doesn't effectively prepare your teammates for the next play. Common between-play language includes phrases like, "nice try", "my bad", or "let's go". The focus is pointed inwards at an individual, instead of looking across the net to analyze your opponent's weaknesses.

To be an effective communicator and team leader, between-play communication should focus on what the opponent is doing. In between rallies, players should direct their attention towards:

- Calling out if the setter is in the front-row so that your team can adjust the defense accordingly if she's an offensive threat;

- Singling out a weak blocker on the other team that should be targeted on offense;

- Distinguishing if there is a strong hitter on the opposing team that needs to be committed to on blocking or adjusted to on defense; and

- Identifying hitter tendencies in a specific rotation.

Note that all of these examples of between-play communication are strategic and succinct. Players shouldn't be worried about sugar coating their message because there isn't time for it. The dialogue should be laser focused on how to make strategic adjustments on the very next play. This is the time setters should be calling out the offensive plays for serve receive, transition balls and free balls. Middle blockers should be identifying the attackers by number across the net. Communication should be direct, concise and focused on the next play.

During-play communication addresses what is happening on the court in the present moment. Here's a few examples of during-play communication:

- Calling the ball loud and early on serve receive to identify who is going to pass the serve;

- Helping your teammates distinguish whether the ball is in or out by following the ball to the line if it's close;

- Identifying a tip early on defense if you're able to read the hitter and see it coming;

- Signaling an audible play in the middle of a rally to target the opposition's weakness when they are out of system.

There is a big difference between strategic court communication and cheerleading. Lack of communication among teammates often stems from players being shy, not knowing what to say, or feeling like it's not their place to speak up. But every position on the court has a key role in team communication. As a player you must learn to make communication a habit.

Effective communication requires players to listen as well as speak up between plays and during rallies. Court communication can be a powerful team-building tool if properly utilized. Learning to improve communication with your teammates will direct your attention outwards and naturally shift your mindset from a "me" to a "team" mentality.

4. Create a culture of belonging

How can you take a roster of over a dozen unique individuals and meld them into a single team with a shared sense of identity and purpose? The answer is that you must create a team culture of *belonging*.

There is a subtle difference between belonging and fitting in. To belong means to find acceptance within a particular group. A team culture of belonging means that you can become a part of something bigger than yourself *and* bring your most authentic self to the court without losing a sense of your core identity. Fitting in means to be socially compatible with the other members of the group. A fitting in culture on a team ostracizes players who are different than the majority and forces assimilation.

Brené Brown, PhD, LMSW, author and research professor at the University of Houston, describes the difference perfectly in an article she wrote for Oprah, "Fitting in, I've discovered during the past decade of research, is assessing situations and groups of people, then twisting yourself into a human pretzel in order to get them to let you hang out with them. *Belonging* is something else entirely—it's showing up and letting yourself be seen and known as you really are—love of gourd painting, intense fear of public speaking and all.[20]"

A culture of belonging starts with belief that every member of the team has an essential role to play. Finding and utilizing the unique assets of each player on your team will optimize your team's potential. Your strengths might complement your teammate's weaknesses and vice versa. The most quiet player on your team might be the best listener. The consistent kill leader on your team might not be a natural leader on the court.

In a private interview with Kevin Hambly, the Head Women's Volleyball Coach at Stanford, I learned that their coaching staff doesn't assign captains to their team. The floor captain is whoever is setting at the time. Coach Hambly looks for natural leadership to emerge in different areas, and then empowers that leadership by amplifying their message. Depending on the composition and needs of the team, they might have a competitive leader, a task leader or a social leader. Every role is recognized as a contributing factor to the team's success.

A culture of belonging also respects the differences between players. To be a great teammate, you don't have to always agree with or even like every member of your team. However you do have to respect them. Respect starts by making a conscious effort to truly see and learn about your teammates.

After the Women's US National Team won the 2014 FIVB Volleyball Women's World Championships in Italy, libero Nicole Davis shared insight into the mental preparation and social dynamic of their winning team, "We believe and we say out loud every day that our team is full of special people, that what we are doing is part of something that is much bigger than ourselves, that we are committed to and doing things the 'right' way, and that we will succeed in reaching our goals for these reasons. Our belief and strength as a group is what won us this World Championship.[21]"

One size never fits all. It just makes people who don't fit the mold feel uncomfortable and unwelcome. To get the best results, we've got to bring our most authentic selves to the court. Dropping your identity to force culture fit will not produce the highest and best performing results. Teams that demand sameness in player personalities, leadership styles and culture may miss out on the greatest contributions that individuals have to offer.

5. Dismantle implicit bias.

Before I explain the strategies for dismantling implicit bias within team culture, I want you to go through a visualization exercise with me. Picture the following scenario.

You walk into a convention center with dozens of volleyball courts. There are games being played on every single court in the complex.

You walk up to a random court and start watching the match. You don't know either of the teams playing, but it looks like an intense game so you watch the match play out.

Number 11 rips a jump serve that's picked up by the receiving team's libero. An on point pass just slightly left of center enables the setter to run a slide to the middle hitter who crushes it down the line.

The referee calls the ball out and one team erupts in anger as the other one rushes towards the center of the court cheering. The match ends with a controversial call by the referee.

While the sidelines and stands are filled with a mix of emotional cheers, the head coach of the losing team charges the referee stand to dispute the call. Meanwhile the assistance coach gathers the players into a huddle to condole them on the tough loss.

Now pause for a minute. Before we continue I want to ask you a few questions about what you visualized.

Was the head coach male or female?

Was the assistant coach male or female?

How many people of color were there on the team? How many coaches, refs, fans, etc. were people of color?

Were the parents in the stands all straight couples? Was there any same-sex couples in the stands? Were there any gender-nonconforming fans?

Were all the fans able-bodied?

Was there any variation in the ethnicity of the fans at all?

You don't have to share your answers with anyone, but you should be aware of them. This exercise is designed to help you become aware of your own *implicit biases* within the context of volleyball. We often don't realize the stereotypes that we live with and perpetuate until someone gets excluded or hurt.

My favorite definition of implicit bias comes from the Kirwan Institute for the Study of Race and Ethnicity, "Implicit bias refers to the attitudes or stereotypes that affect our understanding, actions, and decisions in an unconscious manner. These biases, which encompass both favorable and unfavorable assessments, are activated involuntarily and without an individual's awareness or intentional control.[22]"

Basically we tend to favor other people who look, talk, think and act like us. These feelings and attitudes towards others are often rooted in our childhood experiences. As a result, most of us lack deep relationships with people who differ in race, ethnicity, sexual orientation, age, and socio-economic background. Whether you realize it or not, your implicit bias will likely impact your volleyball career and manifest itself in the form of friendship groups, communication methods, leadership styles and social norms within your team.

In the case of the volleyball match that you envisioned

above, it's likely that you pictured a white male head coach, a female assistant, two teams of cisgender-feminine-presenting players and parents in the stands who are straight and able-bodied. The majority, if not all, of the people you pictured were also probably the same race and ethnicity as yourself.

The first step towards dismantling your tendencies toward implicit bias is to develop consciousness. Lack of awareness is the biggest obstacle to inclusion and integration within a team culture.

The next step is to understand how types of privilege and discrimination impact target groups at varying degrees of intensity. The table below is a graphic representation of common types of identity factors that experience privilege and discrimination.

Types of Identify Factors	Discrimination	Privilege
Gender	Women, transgender people	Men
Racial	People of color	White people
Sexual orientation	Lesbian, gay, bi-sexual	Heterosexual people
Religion	Non-Christian	Christian
Ability	People with	People

	disabilities	without disabilities
Socio-economic status	Poor, working class	Rich, upper class
Immigrant status	Immigrant	US-born
Language	Non-English	English
Marriage status of parents	Divorced	Married

Differences in gender, race, sexual orientation, socio-economic background, ability and so forth, are all factors that make up your whole identity. Your identity factors shape the lens through which you view the world and navigate life.

As teammates and team leaders it's important to understand that integration into the team culture is going to be more difficult for some players than others based upon their identity factors. If your identity factors align with the majority of your teammates, then it's going to take less effort for you to connect with them. That doesn't mean you're a better player or teammate, it just means that you have more privilege.

Before I go any further, I want to clarify what I mean by privilege because the term seems to stir up a lot of different emotions for folks. Privilege does not mean that you've never suffered discrimination or earned something through hard work. My favorite definition of privilege comes from a YouYube video by American comedian Franchesca Ramsey, also known as Chescaleigh. According to Chescaleigh, privilege means, "there are some things in life you won't have to think about because of who you are.[23]"

Let me give you an example that applies to volleyball. Your college team is entering into post season and you're waiting to find out where your NCAA playoff matches will take place. Based upon the win-loss record of your season, it's very unlikely that your team will get a home match. That means your team will probably have to travel to another state to compete. The coaches and most players are only concerned with drawing a team that your team can beat to advance to the next round. However, one player on the team self identifies as a lesbian and therefore is extremely concerned about getting bullied or discriminated against at a location that isn't widely accepting of her sexual orientation or gender-neutral presentation. The concern about bullied had not crossed the minds of any other individual on the team, but for the player that identifies as a lesbian, it's a real threat.

Not having to worry about discrimination on the basis of sexual orientation or race when playing in some parts of the country or the world is an example of privilege.

On a much larger scale, a collective fear of discrimination was experienced by athletes in the 2014 Olympic Games in Sochi, Russia due to the country's law banning "propaganda on nontraditional sexual relationships[24]" which triggered an increase in homophobic violence leading up to the Olympics. While the international Olympic committee (IOC) and the NCAA have written recommended LGBTQI+ inclusive policies, many conferences and schools have not yet adopted the protections.

As a teammate, you may or may not identify with this type of discrimination, but if you want to build a relationship on trust than you've got to learn to recognize instances of discrimination and demonstrate allyship within your team. When players on a team understand, trust and care for one another, they are more receptive to constructive criticism and encouragement. By creating space for individual differences within team culture and leadership, players are much more likely to bring their whole selves to the court and perform at their highest potential. The failure to recognize, honor and celebrate each player's unique differences, is a wasted source of power.

So how do we create a team culture in which all players can bring their whole selves to the volleyball court?

Creating a safe space for everyone starts with creating core values for your team that include everyone. An inclusive team culture is a safe space for each individual to be the most authentic version of their beautifully-unique self. You must make room for one another's differences and affirm each other's identities. It means paying attention to one another's needs, being curious about each other's history, and sensitive to everyone's suffering. And most important of all, you have to build relationships with each other. The most successful team cultures are relationship-based.

Teamwork is all about unifying. The process of transforming a group of individuals into a cohesive team unit is messy and emotional at times. To do that you have to overcome every communication barrier, close every gap, face every fear and set aside every judgement between teammates. At times our job as players, and as leaders, is to step outside of our comfort zones to make space for a teammate to contribute, hold teammates accountable, or have hard conversations. Creating a culture of teamwork isn't easy, but it's vital to the success of every team.

MODULE 6 : SELF-CARE

"It's important to just kind of get away from your sport until you miss it . . . It's about taking time to enjoy other aspects of life or learn new things. It helps rejuvenate.[25]"

Misty May-Treanor, three-time Beach Volleyball Olympic Gold Medalist

Athletes often overlook the importance and value of dedicated self-care. Team schedules typically involve lots of volleyball practices, weight-training and conditioning. On top of that, student athletes also have to prioritize studying and balancing some sort of social life. That doesn't leave much time leftover for self-care. If you don't create space and dedicate time to nurture and care for yourself mentally, emotionally, physically and spiritually, your mind and body are likely to become worn down and burnt-out. Self-care directly correlates to mental-wellness. Just like on an airline when you're asked by flight attendants to secure your own oxygen mask before assisting others, players need to prioritize their own mental wellness before you can effectively support and lead others on your team.

Although the practice of self-care is often neglected on teams, this chapter might be the most important one in this entire book. Here are 4 strategies that will improve your mental-wellness both on and off the court.

8. Yoga as a training tool.

Cross training for volleyball with yoga has all sorts of physical benefits including flexibility, balance and core strength. Yoga teaches athletes to combine physical movements with conscious and patterned breathing, producing a balance between heightened levels of concentration and relaxation. In addition to all the benefits I've already mentioned, there are three components of yoga that really stand out as being especially helpful for volleyball players.

The greatest advantage yoga offers athletes is *proprioception,* an awareness of your body's position in relation to your surroundings, otherwise known as your "sixth sense[26]". In the context of volleyball, proprioception is knowing where your body exists in space in relation to the net, the lines on the court, your teammates and the ball.

You don't need to look at the antennae while you're hitting to know where it is on the net. You're capable of avoiding it without actually bringing it into focus.

As a setter you don't need to look at the net, to set the ball to the target. Even if the pass pulls you out of position, you've got a natural awareness of your body's distance to the net and position on the court.

Your awareness of how quickly you need to swing your arm to make contact with the ball is another example of proprioception.

You can increase your proprioception by doing yoga. Yoga is the practice of body-based consciousness through movement. When you move your body with intention and attention, you develop a greater awareness of your body and everything around you.

The second advantage yoga distinctly offers athletes is the development of mindfulness through movement. Whereas mindfulness is awareness of your experience without judgement, yoga is the physical manifestation of mindfulness. The practice of yoga literally and physically embodies mental fitness.

In Module 4, I covered the benefits of cultivating a consistent mindfulness practice and walked you through a sample 5-minute mindfulness exercise which you can do prior to practice or competition. Adding yoga to your weekly training regime, will teach you how to transfer the practice of mindfulness into action through physical movement. Yoga is an excellent strategy to help you reduce the noise in your mind and build a greater awareness of self and your surroundings when you are being physically active so you can go into competition poised and in control under pressure.

Remember, yoga is a body, mind and breath practice. When you get your body, mind and breath to sync up, your movements on the court will become more efficient and fluid. Syncing your body, mind and breath will also make you feel more at home in yourself and in your role on the team. Body, mind and breath awareness on the court will also drastically improve your ability to release tension under pressure and perform consistently, regardless of external forces.

The third advantage of yoga for athletes, which I find uniquely empowering to player relationships and team building, is the concept of *namaste*. If you have taken any yoga class in the United States, the teacher probably ended class by saying namaste and bowing towards each individual in the room. According to Yoga Journal, in Sanskrit, "*Nama* means bow, *as* means I, and *te* means you. Therefore, *namaste* literally means "bow me you" or "I bow to you.[27]" Oftentimes you'll hear yoga teachers say, "the divine in me, sees and honors the divine in you."

Seeking to fully see and understand the person in front us is a transformative practice. My favorite yoga teacher, Mindy Bacharach, likes to say, "The only difference between the mundane and the sacred is how we pay attention."

Seeing, understanding, accepting and celebrating your

teammates as they are breaks down the tendencies of implicit bias that I discussed in Module 5. When you practice a posture of curiosity and acceptance, you will strengthen the relationships on your team that form the building blocks of teamwork.

There are many more benefits to yoga, but those three – proprioception, mindfulness through movement and the practice of consciously bowing to your teammates (aka *namaste*) are the ones I find most practical and empowering for volleyball players.

Incorporating yoga into your training regimen can be as easy as doing a solo online class in your home, or joining a yoga studio to attend class in a group setting once or twice a week outside of practice. Now more than ever, there are tons of free online yoga classes and apps for athletes to download and practice individually or together as a team.

Regardless of how you choose to incorporate yoga into your training and pre-game routine, keep in mind that learning to develop an awareness of your body and paying attention to your breath is more important than how long or hard you push yourself during any one session. Unlike other aspects of conditioning it's not about pushing yourself to your physical limit, it's about becoming aware of your body and learning how to control your mind in order to navigate your way to peak performance. When you're already playing volleyball, weight lifting, and conditioning, a power-based yoga practice may not be the best choice. A Yin-Yang, or balanced, type restorative practice with an element of meditation is most beneficial for players seeking mind awareness and control.

2. Rest, the unexpected key to resilience.

Roberta Kraus, PhD. is the President of the Center for Sports Psychology in Colorado Springs. She's an expert at helping individual players, coaches and teams develop mental strategies that result in consistently achieving a player's peak performance. The mental training programs that she's designed and implemented have a proven track record of improving player performance, communication and team dynamics under pressure.

She's worked hand in hand with Olympians, Paralympians, college programs and athletic departments to enhance athlete performance through mental training techniques. Listening to her closing presentation at the 2016 AVCA Coaches Convention on *Resilience Tools and Techniques* made me realize one critical piece to world class training that most athletes underestimate the value of or overlook completely – the importance of dedicated recovery time.

According to a poll from the National Alliance for Youth Sports, approximately 70 percent of kids in the United States drop out of sports by time they turn 13 because, "it's just not fun anymore". *Staleness Syndrome* or burn-out starts at a young age and continues to plague players and coaches at every level. Athletes and coaches who overtrain, lack life balance and deny themselves critical space for rest and recovery burn out prematurely.

In other words, those players and coaches lack *resilience*.

Dr. Kraus defines resilience as, "the capacity of a department, team, coach or athlete to maintain their emotional balance, to empathize, to hope and to persist in the face of frustration".

So how do we cultivate healthy patterns and habits within our team to sustain resilience?

The solution is rest.

It's so obvious that it seems unnecessary to explain and yet the problem continues to plague so many players and coaches that it needs to be seriously addressed. Most players live right on the edge of overtraining and under recovering. Giving your body sufficient sleep, food and water are all a critical part of your training regimen. You should prioritize rest as much as you value strength and conditioning training. If you want to stay in the game, you've got to have balance in your training and guard space for your body to recover. Intentional recovery time is a critical component to developing resilience in players and teams.

3. Embrace body positivity.

In the book *U Thrive : How to Succeed in College (and Life)*, the authors Daniel Lerner and Dr. Alan Schlechter expose a wildly inaccurate article published in *Seventeen* magazine back in August, 1989 that changed the way incoming freshman university students would think about their bodies and dorm life. Without the backing of any formal study or scientific evidence, the magazine article claimed that most students gain fifteen pounds during their first year in college.

For decades to follow, fears of gaining the "freshman fifteen" spread among campuses across the nation. Daniel Lerner and Dr. Alan Schlechter report that, "According to a survey of every study on the topic between 1985 and 2008, the average amount of weight gained for college freshmen (who actually do gain weight) is 3.8 pounds. One study showed that up to 36 percent of students ended up weighing *less* by the end of their first year.[28]" Furthermore, the studies showed that the most common factor to weight gain in college was not food, it was alcohol.

Unfortunately, the damage of the magazine article had already been done. The faulty claim cemented the idea of the freshman fifteen into the psyche of college students which triggered a widespread fear of gaining weight among eighteen-year-olds, particularly young women.

In February, 2016, the *Yale Daily News* published an article highlighting the results of a Yale co-authored study which found that 25 percent of female collegiate athletes suffer from disordered eating habits[29]. Interviews with members of all 18 of Yale University women's sports teams, including volleyball, reported at least one member of the team who experienced disordered eating and body image issues during their college careers.

Yale staffer Daniela Brighenti reported that, "For most student-athletes interviewed, societal expectations and pressures on how their bodies should look were the main reason behind their issues with weight and body image.[30]"

Most athletes agree that conditioning workouts and weightlifting routines are pivotal to excelling in their sport, however the problem often arises when female athletes compare their bodies to female non-athletes. Yale volleyball player Lucy Tashman added that, "being on a team helps athletes come to terms with how their bodies look, since the workouts make players better and help the entire team[31]". However, if the results of the Yale study are accurate, a supportive team isn't enough to protect players from the abusive comments, destructive social pressure and nagging insecurities that all female athletes face.

So, how can you embrace body positivity and instill healthy lifestyle habits?

To start with, here's a summarized list of 10 steps you can do to improve your body image. The list below is sourced from the National Eating Disorders Association (NEDA)[32].

- Appreciate all that your body can do.
- Keep a top-ten list of things you like about yourself.
- Remind yourself that "true beauty" is not simply skin-

deep.
- Look at yourself as a whole person.
- Surround yourself with positive people.
- Shut down those voices in your head that tell you your body is not "right" or that you are a "bad" person.
- Wear clothes that are comfortable and that make you feel good about your body.
- Become a critical viewer of social and media messages.
- Do something nice for yourself.
- Use the time and energy that you might have spent worrying about food, calories, and your weight to do something to help others.

Memorizing and reciting mantras or affirmations is another great way to promote self-acceptance of your body. Here's a few that have helped me in my own personal journey to overcome disordered eating:

- My body deserves to be nourished and loved.
- My body is a sacred gift, I want to honor it with love and respect.
- I am more than body; my body does not define my self-worth.

- I choose healing and a healthy lifestyle over restrictive dieting.
- "If I'm shinin', everybody gonna shine. I was born like this, don't even gotta try." – Lizzo, *Juice*.

In the workbook you'll find many more ideas for activities and resources that can help you and your team avoid the dangerous downward spiral of unhealthy and unrealistic body expectations. If this is something you struggle with, please know that you are not alone. There is no shame in suffering through body image sensitivity and disordered eating. I strongly encourage you to be honest about your internal struggle with trusted teammates or friends and seek-out a mental health professional if needed.

It is worth investing the time and emotional energy into recovery. Malnourishment is far more dangerous than you realize. Avoiding meals will eventually cut off relationships to your loved ones and the earth itself. It is possible to eat without feeling the sickness of guilt. Healing may take much longer than you think but you can overcome this battle.

You can enjoy food with loved ones and cherish the things that grow from gardens. Resolving this area of your life might be the most important thing you take away from this book.

4. Find balance.

Volleyball is not your identity. It may be your passion and driving motivation. It may dictate your schedule and determine where you live. Your team may even feel more like your family than your actual family. However, it's important to always remember that volleyball is what you do, not who you are. Winning or losing doesn't define you. Your statistics aren't a reflection of all your skills and qualities. How you play on the court, is not a reflection of your self worth.

That line between player and self often gets blurred when athletes train year-round and travel to compete each weekend. Players are often expected to skip social events and sacrifice time with loved ones on holidays or special occasions. How many of you had to skip prom or play in a volleyball tournament over spring break when your other classmates went on an exotic trip?

If you're playing collegiate volleyball now, or have aspirations to some day, my guess is that you're all too familiar with the sacrifices required to compete at the next level. Sometimes as a player, you're asked to make difficult decisions to prioritize your sport over other aspects of life that are also important to you. It's not easy to balance volleyball, school and life when there's so much pressure to prove your commitment to your sport and your team.

But the reality is that at some point in your life you will stop playing volleyball. It might be an injury that keeps you on the bench or ends your career prematurely. For some student athletes, the weight of academics is too heavy to continue investing in the game. Others of you might have a volleyball career that extends far beyond college and continues professionally at the international level. Either way, at some point in your life, you're going to stop playing.

When that time comes, your life will look very different than it does now. However, there will be aspects of playing a team sport that always stay with you. The friendships with your current teammates may fade, but learning how to work well with others to achieve a mutual goal is an invaluable lesson. Your muscle mass will likely decrease and your vertical jump will definitely decline, but understanding how to develop a healthy lifestyle and workout training regimen will carry you through your life. And if you have learned how to balance the tension between volleyball and the other demands on your time now, you are much more likely to find harmony between work, family and other aspects of your life in the future. Volleyball teaches you numerous skills that are transferable to your academic life and will prove to be invaluable throughout your career in the future.

The lessons you learn through volleyball will last a lifetime. Ten years from now nobody will remember what you did or did not accomplish on the court. It's just a game. Nobody is keeping score on your career. Play it only as long as it's fun, then let it go freely. When the time comes for you to hang up your jersey, give yourself space to grieve the loss of your first true passion. Hold on to the life lessons and friendships gifted by the game.

CLOSING INSPIRATION

"We are all going to fall short. We are going to have some bitter losses, very painful defeats and failures. We have to use those to come back even stronger. That's what makes it sweeter, when we can overcome those and figure out a way to win. The great teams can do that, and those are the gold medal winning teams.[33]"

– KARCH KIRALY, Olympic Gold Medalist in beach and indoor volleyball, and U.S. Women's National Volleyball Team Coach 2012 - present.

When I was in high school I got recruited by several Division 1 schools including the University of Washington and UC Santa Barbara, the school I ultimately committed to. But there was always a piece of me that wanted to play for UCLA like both my parents had back in the 1960's and 70's.

I grew up watching Annett Buckner-Davis and Jenny Johnson Jordan wearing their blue and gold jersey's in Pauley Pavilion. I attended the UCLA volleyball camps each summer hoping to get noticed. I really wanted to be a UCLA Bruin.

When my club coach finally asked Andy Banachowski, the head UCLA women's volleyball coach at the time, if UCLA was interested in recruiting me as a setter, his response left me no hope. "She's just too small to play at the next level", Coach Banachowski said. I was devastated. My dreams felt crushed. It felt like I had been dismissed before even given the chance to prove myself.

Everyone faces moments of defeat in their volleyball career. Sometimes these moments come in the form of personal rejection, when words from a coach or teammate hurt you at your core. Maybe it's an injury or losing your starting spot that triggers a crisis of confidence. For most teams, it comes in the form of an unexpected loss. Whatever the cause, always remember that the darkness will pass and you always have the choice to learn from the pain.

In my case, the only thing I could do to compensate for my 5'4" stature was work on increasing my vertical jump. And so I did. In the face of rejection I dedicated myself to doing extra weight lifting and plyometrics (jump training). I put in extra hours at the gym, on the court and in the sand. When I showed up at UC Santa Barbara as an incoming freshman setter, I was ready to take on a starting role along side four seniors and one junior. I was determined to demonstrate that I could compete at the next level despite my limited height.

UCLA wasn't scheduled to play us that season. However in the 1998 Pacific Regional Final of the NCAA Division I Women's Volleyball Tournament, we drew them in the 2nd round of playoffs my freshman year. It was a home match and the stands were packed. The winner would travel to Wisconsin to compete in the round of Sweet Sixteen. The loser would return home and their season would be over.

I don't remember the details of the match, but I do recall making eye-contact with Coach Banachowski when the final ball hit the floor on match point. We toppled UCLA in a 3-1 victory that night. After the celebration circle winded down, my teammates and I walked towards the net to shake hands with our opponents. When my turn came to shake Coach Banachowski's hand, I looked directly into his eyes and said, "you still think I'm too short?"

So much of individual and team success is contingent upon belief in yourself and having a growth-mindset to improve on the volleyball court. I can't reiterate enough how important it is to dedicate time and energy to training the mental game of volleyball.

Headstrong is the book I wish I'd had when I was a player. If you struggle with distractions, lack self-confidence, or self-destruct during high-pressure matches then you'll definitely want to use the strategies in this book.

This book is about so much more than volleyball. The wisdom and experience I gained from competitively playing a team sport has influenced the principles that guide my life today. I truly believe the bond created among teammates and coaches during the intensity of training and competition is a unique one. All student athletes and coaches forego some aspect of their personal lives for the greater good of the team. We all share the common sacrifice of our social lives for the love of sport. As a result, friendships between players and coaches are one of the greatest gifts of the game.

Back when I was an aspiring 17-year-old volleyball player, I had the honor of receiving setting training from a legendary coach named Harlan Cohen. Standing at no more than 5'6" with a fragile stature, you'd never believe he was the coach who led the US women's national team to a gold medal at the 1967 Pan American Games and a silver medal at the 1967 World Championships in Tokyo. Coach Cohen was a wealth of wisdom on the mental aspects of playing the game that he'd dedicated his life to studying and coaching.

Among all the many valuable and sometimes quirky lessons he taught me, there is one that I've carried with me throughout my life both on and off the court.

"Coaches are going to teach you a lot of different techniques," Harlan instructed me, "don't waste your time arguing with them over which technique is the best. Just think of the techniques as different tools – useful for different situations, and put them in your toolbox. You can never have too many tools in your toolbox."

Coach Cohen's advice is especially applicable to the strategies in this book. There's lots of different types of tools in here. Some may prove to be incredibly useful to you, and others may not resonate as much. But you can never have too many tools in your toolbox.

HEADSTRONG™ MINDSET TRAINING PROGRAM

Want to dive even deeper into volleyball mindset training? As a mindset coach, a former professional volleyball player, a non-profit founder, an Athlete Ally Ambassador and a public speaker, I love sharing my stories and strategies with players and teams. I truly believe they help others learn how to navigate their own path to improvement, empowerment and balance.

As a former player, I understand the demands that student athletes have on their time, career and health. That's why I've designed a Headstrong™ Mindset Training Program specifically for volleyball players and teams. If you liked what you learned in the book and want to build upon these strategies by applying them to your own life and team, then you should check out my live Headstrong™ Mindset Training Program.

I am now offering both individual and team virtual training sessions on all 6 modules covered in the books. To inquire about booking online sessions for you or your team, just email me at:

brooke@headstrongmindset.com or visit my website to learn more: http://headstrongmindset.com/.

ABOUT THE AUTHOR

Brooke Rundle (she/her/hers) is a former professional volleyball player who felt a strong call to empower athletes through performance consulting and inclusive team building. Brooke is currently working on her doctorate in Sport & Performance Psychology at the University of Western States.

As a player, Brooke had an illustrious volleyball career at UC Santa Barbara where she led the Gauchos to the Regional Finals of the Division 1 NCAA Tournament three times. She was Freshman of the Year and 1st Team All Conference in 1998 and went on to be voted All District and All Conference twice. In 2000, she was named an NCAA Division 1 All-American. After her collegiate career, she went on to play volleyball professionally in Slovenia and the Netherlands.

Brooke is also the co-founder and director of a non-profit called the Casa Llanta Fund (http://bringitusa.com/live/casa-llanta-fund/). The Casa Llanta Fund's mission is to empower marginalized communities in Nicaragua, Costa Rica and Puerto Rico by providing access to sports, education, and employment.

She's also the first volleyball Ambassador for the LGBTQI+ non-profit organization Athlete Ally (https://www.athleteally.org/introducing-brooke-rundle/).

Brooke is originally from California, but resides in Denver, Colorado with her wife Hannah.

ACKNOWLEDGMENTS

I'd like to take this chance to thank all the coaches and players who have generously shared their time with me by doing interviews and provided valuable mindset training advice, strategies and tips. This book is most certainly a collection of wisdom from legends of the game. There were so many coaches and players that contributed to my inspiration in writing this book. I have been so fortunate to learn the game through personal stories, conversations and training with some of the greatest players and coaches of the game.

I hope this book helps to preserve the stories of those beautiful volleyball legends. And I hope it inspires future young players to learn, respect and preserve the history of the game.

Thank you for your support every step of the way!

Mom, Dad, Wesley Dean, Brian Heffernan, Harlan Cohen, Stephanie Cox-Gandara, Mike Fitzgerald, Jon Lee, Kathy Gregory, Mike Maas, Courtney Thompson, Misty May-Treanor, Butch May, Debbie Green, Stan

Gosciniak, Brook Coulter, Al Scates, Steve Bain, Jeff Meeker, Rachelle Sherden, Jen Jacobs, Kevin Hambly, John Dunning, Beth Launiere, Sharon Dingman, Jenny McDowell, Kirsten Bernthal Booth and my volleyball family at East Beach.

I would especially like to thank my wife Hannah for encouraging me to keep pursuing my dreams and always reminding me that specificity is key to sharing a universal truth.

Endnotes

[1] Mark, Gloria. August 14, 2019. Episode 7, "Sorry for the Interruptions", Center for Humane Technology | Your Undivided Attention Podcast, http://humanetech.com/wp-content/uploads/2019/08/CHT-Undivided-Attention-Podcast-Ep.7-Pardon-the-Interruptions.pdf.

[2] Titov, Sergey & Steel, Sandy. "Picture of the Game Report 2016", Fédération Internationale de Volleyball (FIVB), Table 1, Page 48, http://www.fivb.org/EN/Volleyball/Documents FIVB_2016_Picture_of_the_Game_report_VB.pdf

[3] Hoffman, Kevin. "Conditioning for volleyball players", Coach & A.D. Your resource for building powerful sports programs, June 8, 2015, https://coachad.com/articles/conditioning-for-volleyball-players/.

[4] Big Ten Network. "Longest Point Ever!?!?!?!? | Big Ten Volleyball." YouTube. Oct 17, 2015, https://www.youtube.com/watch?v=6DO8yOVYXr0.

[5] NCAA Video. "This 1:55 rally is one of college volleyball's top plays of the week and maybe season", October 11, 2019, https://www.ncaa.com/video/volleyball-women/2019-10-11/di-wvol-top-plays.

[6] Wall, Mike. "Seeing Is Everything", Gold Medal Squared, October 11, 2011,

https://www.goldmedalsquared.com/blog/seeing-is-everything/.

[7] Kaplon, Megan. "35 Inspirational Volleyball Quotes We Love", Flo Volleyball, July 13, 2017, https://www.flovolleyball.tv/articles/5067792-35-inspirational-volleyball-quotes-we-love.

[8] Kotler, Steven. "The Science of Peak Human Performance", TIME, April 30, 2014, https://time.com/56809/the-science-of-peak-human-performance/.

[9] APA.org. (2012). What Are The Benefits of Mindfulness? Retrieved from https://www.apa.org/education/ce/mindfulness-benefits.pdf.

[10] Stinson, Adrienne. "What is box breathing?", Medical News Today, June 1, 2018, https://www.medicalnewstoday.com/articles/321805.

[11] Quinn, Elizabeth. "Visualization Techniques for Athletes", Very Well Fit, March 13, 2020, https://www.verywellfit.com/visualization-techniques-for-athletes-3119438.

[12] Dunphy, Marv, "201+ Volleyball Quotes to Inspire and Motivate Your Team", Volleyball Expert, July 25, 2018, https://volleyballexpert.com/volleyball-quotes/.

[13] Wooden, John. "The Pyramid of Success", https://www.thewoodeneffect.com/pyramid-of-success/.

[14] Kemner, Caren, "201+ Volleyball Quotes to Inspire and Motivate Your Team", Volleyball Expert, July 25, 2018, https://volleyballexpert.com/volleyball-quotes/.

[15] Abby Wambach, "Wolfpack: How to Come Together, Unleash Our Power, And Change the Game", 175 5th Avenue, N.Y. 10010, April 2019, page 58.

[16] Olmstead, Heather. "Heather Olmstead Finds Form in Final Four." Season 1, Episode 11., WiSP Sports #431 The WeCoach Podcast, 14 March 2019.

[17] Porath, Christine. "How Rudeness Stops People from Working Together", Harvard Business Review, January 20, 2017, https://hbr.org/2017/01/how-rudeness-stops-people-from-working-together.

[18] Pearnt, Karen M. "Bullying-suicide link explored in new study by researchers at Yale", July 16, 2008, https://news.yale.edu/2008/07/16/bullying-suicide-link-explored-new-study-researchers-yale.

[19] Mike Krzyzewski, Jamie K. Spatola. Beyond Basketball: Coach K's Keywords for Success, Grand Central Publishing, October 23, 2007.

[20] Brown, Brené. "Brené Brown's Top 4 Life Lessons", Oprah.com, 6/14/2012, http://www.oprah.com/inspiration/life-lessons-we-all-need-to-learn-brene-brown#ixzz6IrtJaih8.

[21] Davis, Nicole. "201+ Volleyball Quotes to Inspire and Motivate Your Team", Volleyball Expert, July 25, 2018,

https://volleyballexpert.com/volleyball-quotes/.

[22] Author Unknown. "Understanding Implicit Bias", The Ohio State University Kirwan Institute for the Study of Race and Ethnicity, 2015, http://kirwaninstitute.osu.edu/research/understanding-implicit-bias/.

[23] Ramsey, Franchesca. "5 Tips For Being An Ally." YouTube. November 22, 2014. https://www.youtube.com/watch?v=_dg86g-QlM0.

[24] Herszenhorn, David M. (2013-08-11). "Gays in Russia Find No Haven, Despite Support From the West". The New York Times. Retrieved 10 February 2014.

[25] Kaplon, Megan. "35 Inspirational Volleyball Quotes We Love", Flo Volleyball, Jul 13, 2017, https://www.flovolleyball.tv/articles/5067792-35-inspirational-volleyball-quotes-we-love.

[26] Walker, Elise. "Proprioception: Your Sixth Sense, Why movement and sensation are inextricably linked", Helix Connecting You to Science, Oct 27, 2014, https://helix.northwestern.edu/article/proprioception-your-sixth-sense.

[27] Geno, Rita. "The Meaning of "Namaste"", Yoga Journal, November 12, 2018, https://www.yogajournal.com/practice/the-meaning-of-quot-namaste-quot.

[28] Lerner, Daniel and Schlechter, Dr. Alan. U Thrive : How to Succeed in College (and Life), Published April 18th 2017 by Little, Brown Spark, page 204-205.

[29] Brighenti, Daniela. "Female athletes confront body image", Yale Daily News,February 15, 2016, https://yaledailynews.com/blog/2016/02/15/female-athletes-confront-body-image/.

[30] Brighenti, Daniela. "Female athletes confront body image", Yale Daily News,February 15, 2016, https://yaledailynews.com/blog/2016/02/15/female-athletes-confront-body-image/.

[31] Brighenti, Daniela. "Female athletes confront body image", Yale Daily News,February 15, 2016, https://yaledailynews.com/blog/2016/02/15/female-athletes-confront-body-image/.

[32] National Eating Disorders Association. (n.d.). 10 steps to positive body image. NEDA: Feeding Hope. Retrieved from https://www.nationaleatingdisorders.org/learn/general-information/ten-steps.

[33] Kiraly, Karch. "35 Inspirational Volleyball Quotes We Love", Flo Volleyball, July 13, 2017, https://www.flovolleyball.tv/articles/5067792-35-inspirational-volleyball-quotes-we-love.